Who Are We Really?:
Latin American Family, Local and Micro-Regional Histories, and Their Impact on Understanding Ourselves

SALALM Secretariat
Latin American Library
Tulane University

Who Are We Really?: Latin American Family, Local and Micro-Regional Histories, and Their Impact on Understanding Ourselves

Papers of the Fifty-Ninth Annual Meeting of the
SEMINAR ON THE ACQUISITION OF
LATIN AMERICAN LIBRARY MATERIALS

Salt Lake City, Utah
May 10–14, 2014

Roberto C. Delgadillo
Editor

SALALM Secretariat
Latin American Library
Tulane University

The views of the authors are their own and do not represent
the official views of SALALM, its officers, or agents.

ISBN: 0-917617-92-4

Contents

Preface and Acknowledgements

When I think back on the first Seminar on the Acquisition of Latin American Library Materials (SALALM) meeting I attended, in June 2002 at Cornell University, I still feel the warmth of meeting new colleagues and subsequent friends, who shared a deep and solid interest in the trends and traditions of Latin American librarianship. In the days that followed I was treated as a family member, exposed to formats and strategies employed by librarians and their associated institutions, and to *libreros* who affirmed the values, goals, and vision of SALALM's mission statement. That sense of family never left me, so it is not difficult to see what inspired the theme of the 59th SALALM meeting of May 10–14, 2014, at the Radisson Downtown in Salt Lake City, Utah. That theme was "Who Are We Really?: Latin American Family, Local and Micro-Regional Histories, and Their Impact on Understanding Ourselves."

The present volume includes a representative sample of the presentations made at the conference, and captures the essence of how scholars and librarians focus on family, local and micro-regional historical resources, and their place in the scholarship. Further, the scholarship explores several areas. One is how these resources add to the discussion of genealogical data: how families represent themselves; and how governments record vital statistics to document growth of population, guarantee certain rights for citizens, as well as attempt to document non-citizens. Another area treats racial and ethnic identities, or how people view themselves and are viewed by others. Still another is how those perceived identities conflict with perceptions of governments in the citizenship and rights guaranteed to people based on racial and ethnic identities.

What this volume does not capture, and can only be experienced in person, is the warm, informal sharing of information among libreros, experienced librarians, new SALALM members, and scholars. It is in this that SALALM comes together and why we look forward to seeing one another annually, when possible.

I want to thank many people and institutions who helped organize the SALALM meeting. I am very indebted to John Wright and the Local Arrangements Committee, and especially Wendy Duran at the Harold B. Lee Library, for their collective expert logistical assistance. Salt Lake City, Utah, was a wonderful conference site. I am also very grateful to Brigham Young University for its commitment to making our meeting a success. An immense thanks to Orchid Mazurkiewicz and the Editorial Board for their help in editing these papers. I want to express my gratitude to the SALALM Secretariat, as well, for its efficient efforts and helpfulness. Thanks also to the many active members of SALALM who participated in committee meetings and volunteered as panelists, moderators, and rapporteurs. Finally, I dedicate these proceedings to Lynn Shirey, with whom I shared a taxi ride following the end of the 2001 Feria Internacional del Libro de Guadalajara, and who strongly encouraged me to attend SALALM. Needless to say, my SALALM membership has been the best professional decision in my career!

Roberto C. Delgadillo

1. From the Colony to the Republic: Bibliographic Notes on Entrepreneurial Dynasties in Cuba from 1800 to 1958

Rafael E. Tarragó

There was a Cuban proverb used during the early part of the twentieth century: "Abuelo bodeguero, hijo caballero y nieto pordiosero" (the grandfather's a shopkeeper; the son's a gentleman; and the grandson's a pauper). It referred to the alleged incapability of Spanish settlers and their Cuban descendants to accumulate capital across generations, and to create entrepreneurial dynasties in either merchant financing or agricultural manufacturing. Contrary to what that proverb says, at least some Spaniards in Cuba accumulated capital, and their descendants were able to preserve and sometimes increase what they had inherited (Moreno Lázaro 2013, 43–78).

The purpose of this paper is to highlight sources of information about the members of the Cuban oligarchy from 1800 to 1958, in order to learn who they were. Much of the literature reviewed consists of books and articles on general economic history. These include chapters on, or make extensive reference to, Spanish and Cuban entrepreneurs and the family enterprises that they founded in Cuba.

Finding the Names of Cuban Entrepreneurial Dynasties

Hugh Thomas (1971) often refers to the Cuban oligarchy in his massive history of Cuba from 1762 to 1970, *Cuba, or, The Pursuit of Freedom*. Its appendix lists the names of Cuban entrepreneurs who lived in the 1700s and the most prominent members of the clans that they founded. Most of the genealogies in that appendix (of the Montalvos, the Pedroso-Herrera-Recios, the Arango-Núñez Castillos, the O'Farrills, and the Calvo-Peñalver-O'Reilly-Las Casas) do not go beyond the nineteenth century. However, those of the Montalvos and the O'Farrills extend to the 1950s (Thomas 1971, 1496–1507). Mercedes García Rodríguez (2007, 340–59) includes a list of families as an appendix (Anexo 4) to her book *Entre haciendas y plantaciones: Orígenes de la manufactura azucarera en La Habana*.

Who Are We Really?: Latin American Family, Local and Micro-Regional Histories, and Their Impact on Understanding Ourselves. Papers of the Fifty-Ninth Annual Meeting of SALALM, 2014.

Los propietarios de Cuba 1958, by Guillermo Jiménez (2006), is a biographical dictionary. Its entries consist of 551 biographical vignettes of the most powerful and influential people in Cuba in 1958. Each entry indicates the branch of the Cuban economy in which the individual was active and information on associates, both of which help identify family businesses. Most of the individuals represented in this work were active in the sugar industry and banking, but a considerable number were involved in enterprises unrelated to sugar production, such as cigar making, brewing and distilling, mining, raising cattle, broadcasting, and telecommunications (ix). For example, the entry for Julio Lobo indicates the properties he owned, and that he was the second generation of his family doing business in Cuba. Lobo's fortune was the largest on the Island, which proved he had entrepreneurial acumen. His biography does not conform to the stereotype of the second generation, according to the proverb mentioned at the beginning of this essay. He was not an indolent "gentleman" living off the capital created by his hardworking immigrant father (317).

Another work by Guillermo Jiménez (2000), even more useful in identifying multigenerational family businesses in Cuba, is *Las empresas de Cuba 1958*. This dictionary of enterprises is a handy reference tool for the analysis of Cuba's economy and society from the end of the nineteenth century to 1958. It shows that while Cuban capitalism developed financially through a cruel slavery system, it was dynamic, bold, and looked outward to global technologies and markets (7). Listed in alphabetical order, each entry includes the name of a business owner in 1958, and the history of his or her business, including information on restructuring and reorganization, if applicable (14). Such histories reveal whether or not an enterprise was owned by an entrepreneurial dynasty (235).

Carlos del Toro's (2003) *La alta burguesía cubana, 1920–1958* is also useful for identifying prominent names among the entrepreneurial families in Cuba before 1959. This work is a Marxist analysis of the Cuban oligarchy, and explains how family name, place of residence, education, and prestige are part of bourgeois accumulation of wealth and development of business relations. However, unlike other analyses of its kind, it names specific individuals and families in order to illustrate class dynamics. For example, at the end of the section on family and gender in the first chapter, the author lists the marriage connections of the Rionda Álvarez family, beginning with Bernardo de la Rionda Álvarez and his marriage to Josefa Polledo Mata (10). The second half of this work, titled "Dinámica socioclasista," is divided into chapters, each focusing on an economic sector or profession (127–301).

The Cuban Oligarchy and the Project for a *Cuba Grande*

In the last quarter of the eighteenth century, some Cuban families of Spanish descent began to accumulate capital through enterprises that processed agricultural products (tobacco), and manufactured food products (sugar). Some of those families preserved their capital across several generations.

On April 10, 1795, Luis de las Casas, governor of Cuba, presided over a meeting of fourteen Cuban-born Spaniards. That was the first meeting of the Junta Económica y de Gobierno del Real Consulado de la Habana, an organization instrumental in the development of Cuba as an export economy. Dominique Gonçalves's (2003) analytical article, "Los doce primeros años de la Junta Económica y de Gobierno del Real Consulado de La Habana," examines this meeting and the individuals who attended it (171). One was Francisco de Arango y Parreño, who was a brilliant advocate for improving agricultural methods, introducing new technologies developed abroad, and experimenting with the cultivation of crops new to Cuba, such as hemp for the production of linen, and cotton. However, Arango y Parreño was foremost a champion of the cultivation of sugar cane and the manufacture of sugar on the Island (Arango y Parreño 1936, 21–113).

Sugar production on a grand scale became a great opportunity for the enrichment of Cuban planters, the merchants in whose ships their sugar was imported, and the Spanish monarchy, to whom all of them paid taxes. The position of Cuba as the largest sugar producer in the Caribbean was established after the slaves of the French colony of Saint-Domingue revolted against their masters and burned their sugar crops and mills (Gonçalves 2003, 172). Cuba became part of a global market, mostly of a single product or monoculture, although in the course of the nineteenth century it also began to export coffee, copper, and tobacco for that market. The history of this process, including the influence on it by Francisco de Arango y Parreño and other Cubans among the entrepreneurial elite, is analyzed in the articles compiled by González Ripoll, et al. (2009) in *Francisco de Arango y la invención de la Cuba azucarera*.

The Junta Económica y de Gobierno was not the only institution in late eighteenth-century Cuba that advocated for technological development and economic growth. The economic societies of Santiago de Cuba and of Havana (founded in 1787 and 1791, respectively) also promoted those advances (Shafer 1956, 151–52, 178–98). Economic societies likewise represented the planter and merchant elite. In her article " 'Clase', poder y matrimonio: Configuración de una élite dirigente: La Sociedad Económica de Cuba de Amigos del País," Lucía Provencio Garrigós (1994) argues that members of that society intermarried with strategic economic and social ends (49–90).

Both the Junta Económica and the Sociedad Económica of Havana were instrumental in bringing the railroad to Cuba. Gert J. Oostindie (1984) has written the definitive account of this achievement in his article, "La burguesía cubana y sus caminos de hierro, 1830–1868." He remarks that Cuba was one of the first places in the world to have a railroad and gives credit for this to the

independent spirit of the Cuban elite and their interest in introducing technological innovations to the Island (99–115).

Merchants and the Growth of Financial Capital
in Nineteenth-Century Cuba

In the first half of the nineteenth century some merchants in Cuba accumulated capital on a grand scale, backed Cuban-born planters, and became the
cofounders of entrepreneurial dynasties. Roland T. Ely (1961) tells the story of
two such merchants of that period in his book, *Comerciantes cubanos del siglo
XIX*. The Englishman, James Drake, settled in Cuba during the last decade
of the eighteenth century. He married a Cuban, Carlota del Castillo, with
whom he had a large family. He also made a fortune in trade through his "Casa
Drake." His son, Carlos Drake, went to Spain and became Count de Vega Mar
through marriage. However, his other son, Santiago, stayed in Havana where
he invested in a horse-driven bus line between downtown Havana and Puentes
Grandes, and established a steamer line at Sagua la Grande (53–101). At a
young age, the Venezuelan, Tomás Terry (1806–1886) settled in Cienfuegos
on the southern coast of Central Cuba. He married Teresa Dorticós, daughter
of one of the city's founders. By 1859, he had acquired two sugar cane plantations, "La Caridad" and "La Esperanza." In the 1880s he began to invest
outside Cuba. It seems that his sons, Francisco and Emilio, were adept entrepreneurs. So were their successors, for as late as 1960 the Terry family was
known for its wealth and influence in Cienfuegos (103–38).

Alejandro García Álvarez (2014) makes extensive reference to entrepreneurs in Cuba in his article, "Dinámica empresarial de los capitales hispano-
cubanos" (260). Ángel Bahamonde and José Cayuela (1992) include extensive
chapters on several founders of entrepreneurial dynasties in their analysis of the
networks of trade and investment created by Spanish merchants in Cuba, *Hacer
las Américas: Las élites coloniales españolas en el siglo XIX*. Sometimes such
dynastic ownership was not by direct descent, but through nephews whom
they brought from Spain to help them run their businesses. One such merchant
was Julián Zulueta y Amondo, whose biography by Eduardo Marrero Cruz
(2006) is one of the few about Cuban entrepreneurs that seem to exist. Julián
Zulueta was born in a town of the Basque province of Álava in 1814. In 1838
he settled in Cuba, went to work for an uncle, and by 1845 owned a sugar mill
named "El Regalado," which he modernized and renamed "Álava." However,
Zulueta's largest source of income was the illegal slave trade. He laundered
his ill-gotten gains and, in 1864, he purchased another mill, "España." He was
a councilman in Havana's *cabildo* or city council, where he influenced urban
development and the commercial and social affairs of the capital city (Marrero
Cruz 2006, 28–32).

The Survival of Cuban Entrepreneurial Dynasties and the Beginnings of Family Manufacturing Businesses in Cuba, 1878–1898

During the Cuban War of Independence of 1868–1878, planters and sugar manufacturers who joined or indirectly supported the separatist cause had their properties confiscated and sold to the highest bidder by the Cuban colonial government. Spanish merchants, who had accumulated capital on a grand scale, purchased those confiscated properties and thus gained social standing associated with owning land. Because of this development it has been mistakenly surmised that after 1878 the landed gentry in Cuba was made up only of native Spaniards. Actually, between 1878 and 1895, many Cuban-born entrepreneurs and landowning families prospered, although many more went bankrupt because of economic crises and changes in the global market for sugar and other Cuban commodities. Two prominent examples of those who prospered were Cuban millionaires, Marta Abreu (1845–1909) and José Emilio Terry (1853–1911).

The restructuring of the sugar industry during those years brought about centralization, a reduction in the number of sugar mills, and greater productivity from those that remained in operation. Similar developments took place in the cigar-making industry. United States tariffs against Cuban cigars kept them out of the US market. By 1866 many cigar factories closed in Cuba but some that remained open were purchased by British capitalists. One of those factories was the renowned "Partagás." Still other Cuban cigar factory owners transferred their operations to the United States, where they employed Cuban immigrants to roll cigars from tobacco leaves imported from Cuba. Two of those *maquiladora* owners were Spaniards. Vicente Martínez Ybor opened a factory outside Tampa, where Ybor City developed, and Carlos Hidalgo Gato opened his in Key West (Stubbs 1989, 30–32).

In the last quarter of the nineteenth century, small manufactures unrelated to commodities began to develop in Cuba. That was the case of the ice-making plant owned by the Herrera family. Ramón Herrera arrived in Cuba in 1829 and eventually got into the shipping business. His nephews established an ice-making plant in 1888, and their descendants expanded to beer brewing and soft drink production. The brothers José and Juan Crusellas Vidal immigrated to Cuba in the 1860s and opened both a candle factory and a lubricant oil plant near Havana. Before the end of the century they were producing soap. José and Juan were succeeded by two nephews, Ramón and Juan Crusellas Faurá, who in 1897 began to produce a laundry soap under the brand name Candado. By the 1950s it was the best-selling laundry soap in Cuba. The brothers Cabrisas Caymaris arrived in Cuba in the 1830s and 1840s and began a shoe making plant, which their nephew Antonio Cabrisas Abasolo inherited before the end of the nineteenth century. María Antonia Marqués Dolz (2002) discusses those developments in her book, *Las industrias menores: Empresarios y empresas en Cuba (1880–1920)*, an excellent analysis of how medium sized enterprises developed in Cuba.

Entrepreneurial Dynasties in the Early Republic of Cuba, 1902–1933

The 1895 Cuban War of Independence ended in 1898 with the US intervention and eventual occupation. That war destroyed a huge amount of property. Cuban sugar mill and plantation owners who had capital invested abroad, such as philanthropist and supporter of the separatist movement, Marta Abreu, could reinvest in their devastated properties. Nevertheless, most were not so fortunate and had to sell their properties to United States corporations. Founded in 1902, the Cuban Republic was a *de facto* economic dependency of the United States because of the conditions imposed by the US government in exchange for the republic's creation and an end to the US military occupation of the Island. It was also due to a treaty of economic reciprocity that forced Cuba to open its markets to all United States products, in exchange for reduced import tariffs for Cuban raw sugar and tobacco leaf. Spaniards in Cuba adapted to the new times and the new hegemon.

The Cuba Cane Sugar Corporation was established in New Jersey on December 31, 1915, with an authorized capital of $50 million. Its shares were underwritten by a private investment banking syndicate managed by J. W. Seligman. The president of this new corporation was Manuel Rionda y Polledo. He is the subject of a biography by Muriel McEvoy (2003), who analyzed the man, his times, and his legacy. After immigrating to Cuba in 1870 when he was sixteen years old and working with his uncle Joaquín Polledo Álvarez, he became a partner in what became Polledo, Rionda y Cía. By 1875, he had married Elina de la Torriente, whose father, Cosme de la Torriente, was the patriarch of a family business empire. Manuel lived until 1943, believing that Cuba was destined to make sugar because her fertile fields were amenable to producing the cane, and because the world's largest sugar consumer was only ninety miles away (282). By that time his sister's son, Higinio Fanjul Rionda, had inherited his trust.

The belief that Cuba was destined to produce sugar for the United States market, an opinion held not only by Manuel Rionda but shared by many Cubans, was summarized by the expression, *"Sin azúcar no hay país,"* or "Without sugar, there's no country." In his book entitled with that phrase, Antonio Santamaría García (2001) analyzed the Cuban economy between the years 1919 and 1939. He concluded that, given conditions during that time, the Cubans who opted for monoculture made a rational decision. Indeed, after the initial recovery of the sugar industry in the first decade of the Republic of Cuba, the vast market of the United States opened for unrefined Cuban sugar. After US demand stabilized, World War I increased the need for it in Europe, where sugar beet manufacturing was disrupted. That ever-growing demand encouraged Cuban producers to reinvest and produce more.

However, in 1920 the sugar beet industry in Europe recovered and regained its domestic markets, so Cuban-based producers found themselves without buyers. It was this crisis that caused many American companies to divest themselves of Cuban sugar manufacturing. At the same time, in order to bring stability to the sugar market, a new treaty of reciprocity was being negotiated between the Cuban and United States governments. Ambitious Cuban capitalists began buying sugar businesses from their United States owners. The economic and political crisis that began in 1930 was exacerbated by another that brought down the administration of dictatorial President General Gerardo Machado in 1933 (Aguilar 1972).

By the end of this period, small manufacturing enterprises begun in Cuba during the last quarter of the nineteenth century became well established, making the Cuban economy different from those of other "sugar islands" of the Caribbean (Marqués Dolz 2002, 1). At the same time, the Cuban tobacco industry recovered, thanks to a growing internal market for cigarettes and to the development of a luxury niche in the global market for handmade cigars (Stubbs 1989, 55; 18). However, the motor of the Republic's economy was the sugar industry. Mary Speck (2005) dedicates a section of her article, "Prosperity, Progress, and Wealth: Cuban Enterprise during the Early Republic, 1902–1927," to Cuban sugar barons.

Entrepreneurial Dynasties in Cuba from 1934 to 1958

The economic and political crisis that brought down General Machado's administration also brought about a revolution in Cuba, for the country had been irreversibly changed after his demise. Workers had become organized and their interests had to be considered by the Cuban government. In order to contain radical unrest in Cuba, the United States unilaterally abrogated the amendment that it had imposed on the Island as a condition to grant it independence in 1902. The US also signed an economic treaty with Cuba in 1934, guaranteeing a quota of its market to Cuban sugar producers. Although this treaty encouraged monoculture and dependence on a single market, it was a godsend for the Cuban entrepreneurs who had purchased sugar mills from Americans. Among them were Julio Lobo, Manuel Aspurn San Pedro, Marcelino García Beltrán, and Francisco Blanco Calás (García Álvarez 2004, 272–89).

Although the United States continued looming as a hegemon in this period, a nationalist spirit rekindled in the 1930s among the Cuban intelligentsia and some in the economic elite. They resented that their country was in the shadow of its powerful northern neighbor, wanted a more independent stance for Cuba in the world, and embraced a Cuban identity based on Hispanic and African cultural elements, as distinct from the Anglo-Saxon culture dominant in the US. Although Cubans of all socioeconomic levels enjoyed American popular culture, as represented by Hollywood films and the music of the bands of the 1940s, Cuban radio stations broadcast traditional Cuban dance music like *sones* and *guarachas*. They also played commercial dance music of Cuban vintage, such as *mambos*, *boleros*, and in the 1950s, *chachachás*. Cuban broadcasting and telecasting companies and their owners were wealthy and influential.

Throughout the Island people moved from rural areas to urban settlements, and this demographic change gave origin to transportation companies, most of them operated by Cuban entrepreneurs. Urbanization increased demand for durable consumer goods, and processed foods, such as condensed milk. Urban dwellers wanted soft drinks, beer, and spirits. Among the Cuban alcohol producers, Compañía Ron Bacardí was the largest in the 1950s. Nicolás Torres Hurtado said that after sugar and tobacco, Bacardí Rum was the best known Cuban product in the world (1982, 10).

Facundo Bacardí went to Cuba in the 1840s, settling in Santiago de Cuba, where he married Amalia Moreau. In 1862 he and José León Boutellier purchased the Núñez distillery and began making what they called "Bacardí Rum." Their product received its first prize at an international industrial fair, the "World's Fair," in Philadelphia in 1876. Facundo's Cuban son, Emilio Bacardí Moreau, was a supporter of independence from Spain and was elected mayor of Santiago de Cuba after the Republic of Cuba was established in 1902. The Compañía Ron Bacardí was a family operation, although an extremely wealthy and dynamic one. It is the only Cuban company about which books have been written. I have located four of them, ranging from a very informative, pamphlet-sized company history by Nicolás Torres Hurtado (1982), *Orígenes de la Compañía Ron Bacardí*, to a book-length family biography by Tom Gjelten (2008), *Bacardi and the Long Fight for Cuba*. In London, Hernando Calvo Ospina (2000) published a scathing history, *Bacardi: The Hidden War*. He describes it as "the story of the close-knit relationship between major stockholders and directors of Bacardí rum, the extreme right wing Cuban American National Foundation, and the CIA… a nasty multi-national corporation acting with impunity against desperate people struggling to improve their lives" (xi). Ursula L. Voss's (2006) *Los Bacardí: Una familia entre el ron y la revolución cubana* is an honest, impartial attempt to record the history of the Bacardí family and their business operations.

In 1958 Cuba's economy was dominated by the sugar industry, banking, and import trade. Outside those sectors, only the electric and telephone companies, two railroad companies, the airline company, two or three mining companies, and Compañía Ron Bacardí, had similar importance. Manufacturing was done mostly by small companies (Jiménez 2000, 16). In 1952, in the journal, *Current History,* Myron S. Heidingsfield published the article, "Cuba: A Sugar Economy," in which he said that of all Latin American countries, Cuba probably enjoyed one of the highest per capita incomes (153). In the same article, however, he decried that the Cuban economy was dominated by the sugar industry. Nevertheless, even some of the smaller industries in Cuba were of considerable size, and the industrial sector grew in the years between 1948 and 1958 (Marqués Dolz 1995, 69–76). In all economic sectors there were family-owned corporations. Learning about those families and their histories allows us to better understand how their corporations were formed.

Conclusions

In the research process for this paper, it struck me that there were relatively few studies about the Cuban oligarchy, its specific entrepreneurial dynasties, or the individuals who founded them. Hopefully this bibliographic essay will be useful to economic historians interested in such families and individuals.

Given the limited number of printed monographic sources on the topic, the researcher should consult Cuban newspapers published in the nineteenth and twentieth centuries. In order to find first-hand information about the goals and worldviews of members of the Cuban oligarchy, the publications should have had Island-wide circulation, such as Havana's *Diario de la Marina*, as well as the *Revista Cubana*, published by the Economic Society of Havana. The weeklies, *Bohemia* and *Carteles,* would be useful for research on the years 1905 to 1958. Researchers should also consult the major newspapers of Santiago de Cuba, Cienfuegos, and Matanzas. However, their best sources would be the institutional archives created by those entrepreneurs, their companies, and the private papers of their family members in library collections in Cuba and abroad.

REFERENCES

Aguilar, Luis. 1972. *Cuba 1933*. Ithaca, NY: Cornell University Press.

Arango y Parreño, Francisco de. 1936. *De la factoría a la colonia*. Habana: Publicaciones de la Secretaría de Educación. Dirección de Cultura.

———. 1979. "Informe del síndico en el expediente instruido por el Consulado de La Habana sobre los medios que conviene proponer para sacar la agricultura y el comercio de la Isla del Apuro en que se hallan." In *Pensamiento de la ilustración: Economía y sociedad iberoamericanas en el siglo XVIII*, edited by José Carlos Chiaromonte. Caracas: Biblioteca Ayacucho.

Bahamonde, Angel, and Jose Cayuela. 1992. *Hacer las Americas: Las elites coloniales españolas en el siglo XIX*. Madrid: Alianza Editorial.

Calvo Ospina, Hernando. 2000. *Bacardi: The Hidden War*. Translated by Stephen Wilkinson and Alasdair Holden, Preface by James Petras. London: Pluto Press.

Ely, Roland T. 1961. *Comerciantes cubanos del siglo XIX*. Bogota: Aedita Editores.

García Álvarez, Alejandro. 2004. "Dinámica empresarial de los capitales hispano-cubanos." *Op. Cit.: Boletín del Centro de Investigaciones Históricas* 15: 245–89.

García Rodríguez, Mercedes. 2007. *Entre haciendas y plantaciones: Orígenes de la manufactura azucarera en La Habana*. Habana: Editorial de Ciencias Sociales.

Gjelten, Tom. 2008. *Bacardi and the Long Fight for Cuba*. New York: Viking.

Gonçalves, Dominique. 2003. "Los doce primeros años de la Junta Económica y de Gobierno del Real Consulado de La Habana." In *Comercio y poder en América colonial: Los consulados de comerciantes, siglos XVII–XIX*, edited by Bernd Hansberger and Jaime Ibarra. Madrid: Iberoamericana.

González Ripoll, María Dolores and Izaskun Álvarez Cuartero, eds. 2009. *Francisco de Arango y la invención de la Cuba azucarera*. Salamanca: Ediciones Universidad de Salamanca.

Heidingsfield, Myron S. 1952. "Cuba: A Sugar Economy." *Current History* 22:150–55.

Jiménez, Guillermo. 2000. *Las empresas de Cuba 1958*. Miami: Ediciones Universal.

———. 2006. *Los propietarios de Cuba 1958*. Habana: Editorial de Ciencias Sociales.

Marqués Dolz, María Antonia. 1995. "The Nonsugar Industrial Bourgeoisie and Industrialization in Cuba, 1920–1959." *Latin American Perspectives* 22 (4): 59–80.

———. 2002. *Las industrias menores; Empresarios y empresas en Cuba (1880–1920)*. Habana: Editora Política.

Marrero Cruz, Eduardo. 2006. *Julián Zulueta y Amondo: promotor del capitalismo en Cuba*. Habana: Ediciones Unión.

Moreno Lázaro, Javier. 2013. " 'Padre bodeguero, hijo caballero': Capital social y periplo empresarial de los españoles en Cuba, 1898–1958." *Revista de Historia Industrial* 51: 43–78.

McAvoy, Muriel. 2003. *Sugar Baron: Manuel Rionda and the Fortunes of Pre-Castro Cuba*. Gainesville: University Press of Florida.

Oostindie, Gert J. 1984. "La burguesía cubana y sus caminos de hierro, 1830–1868." *Boletín de Estudios Latinoamericanos y del Caribe* 37: 99–115.

Provencio Garrigós, Lucía. 1994. " 'Clase', poder y matrimonio: Configuración de una elite dirigente; La Sociedad Económica de Cuba de Amigos del País." *Contrastes: Revista de Historia Moderna* 9:49–90.

Santamaría García, Antonio. 2001. *Sin azúcar no hay país: La industria azucarera y la economía cubana (1919–1939)*. Sevilla: Secretariado de Publicaciones de la Universidad de Sevilla; Consejo Superior de Investigaciones Científicas.

Shafer, Robert Jones. 1958. *The Economic Societies in the Spanish World (1763–1821)*. Syracuse: Syracuse University Press.

Speck, Mary. 2005. "Prosperity, Progress, and Wealth: Cuban Enterprise during the Early Republic, 1902–1927." *Cuban Studies* 36:50–86.

Stubbs, Jean. 1989. *Tabaco en la periferia: El complejo agro-industrial cubano y su movimiento obrero, 1860–1959*. Habana: Editorial de Ciencias Sociales.

Thomas, Hugh. 1971. *Cuba, or, The Pursuit of Freedom*. New York: Harper & Row Publishers.

Toro, Carlos del. 2003. *La alta burguesía cubana, 1920–1958*. Habana: Editorial de Ciencias Sociales.

Torres Hurtado, Nicolás. 1982. *Orígenes de la Compañía Ron Bacardí*. Santiago de Cuba: Editorial Oriente.

Voss, Ursula L. 2006. *Los Bacardí: Una familia entre el ron y la revolución cubana*. México, D.F.: Random House Mondadori, S.A. de C.V.

2. Linkages, Lineage, and Kinship in the Anglo-Caribbean Family Experience: A Genealogical Case Study

Judith E. Toppin

Introduction

The study of the social structure of societies has been undertaken by social anthropologists for decades. To do so effectively, cultural traits and practices are examined. Invariably, this leads to a more complete appreciation of how the society functions. A major component of anthropological research includes the analysis of a society's lineage, kinship patterns, and cultural traits. These areas also fall within the scope of genealogical research. Genealogy is essentially "a line of descent traced continuously from an ancestor" and "the identification, examination and collection of names, events, dates and the corresponding relationships" (Pearsall 1998, 763). The genealogists endeavor to trace family lineage by consulting official records which capture the rites of passage—birth, marriage, and death—and by so doing, place individuals historically in a specific place and time. This clearly shows the interlocking and supportive nature of the disciplines of anthropology and genealogy in relation to the study of society, culture, and kinship patterns. In the early 1900s, anthropologists introduced the collection of genealogical data as part of the research process as it proved beneficial to the study of societies and kinship. Today it is regarded as an essential component of research and described as a "technique of anthropology which involves collecting and compiling pedigrees into tables of genealogy in order to determine kinship systems and the nature of institutions" (Winick 1977, 358).

The collection of genealogical information requires the identification and consultation of both primary and secondary sources. This material can be arranged under two main headings: data collection via an oral method or from written sources (Pine 2015). In the early twentieth century, genealogical researchers focused on tracing lineage based on the availability of written records. Emphasis was given to identifying family crests and coats of arms as these were considered essential aspects of genealogy. While seeking to establish a pedigree line is one approach, contemporary genealogical research

Who Are We Really?: Latin American Family, Local and Micro-Regional Histories, and Their Impact on Understanding Ourselves. Papers of the Fifty-Ninth Annual Meeting of SALALM, 2014.

encourages enquiry into the lives of ancestors who straddle the social strata and cultures, and are both Western and non-Western in origin. The availability of written records provides essential support to family research by revealing lineage and kinship linkages. Additionally, capturing the oral, nonwritten account is also an important part of the research process and is critical to the collection and documentation of family information on non-Western societies. Family stories are passed orally from one generation to another, thereby ensuring the survival of information on kinship and lineage. This use of an oral account is ably illustrated in Alex Haley's publication *Roots,* which documents his family's history from an oral account of the capture, transport, and enslavement of his ancestor in America. This story is retold and passed on to several generations of Haley's family. When tracing his ancestry in Africa, the *griots* in the Gambia, responsible for preserving the oral record of families, recount the circumstances of Haley's ancestor's disappearance, thereby supporting the oral account which had been passed down from one generation to another. The survival of this record allowed him to successfully trace his ancestry back to a village in Africa (Haley 1978, 8, 626, 629).

The *New Oxford Dictionary of English* defines culture as "the attitudes and behavior characteristic of a particular social group" (Pearsall 1998, 447). Anglo-Caribbean culture is a blend of those attitudes, behaviors, and customs of peoples from three continents: Europe, Africa, and Asia. The socioeconomic factors which led to their relocation to the Caribbean contributed to the blending of those cultures which gave rise to contemporary Caribbean society and culture.

The countries categorized as the Anglo-Caribbean are all former British colonies and share similar social, economic, and cultural experiences.[1] Geographically, the region includes islands and mainland territories. It stretches from Belize in Central America, continues southward in an arc shape, and incorporates all the English-speaking islands in the Caribbean Sea until it reaches Trinidad and Tobago. Guyana, the only English-speaking country in South America, is also included in one definition of the Anglo-Caribbean. The territories were originally inhabited by Amerindians, but since the arrival of Christopher Columbus in 1492, they became home to Europeans, African slave labor and, later, Asian and European indentured laborers. The economies of the regions were agriculturally based and, at varying times, cultivated the cash crops of tobacco, sugar, bananas, and cocoa.

Tracing Anglo-Caribbean ancestral lineage can be challenging if the researcher does not have an appreciation of the social, cultural, and economic issues which influenced the lives of the inhabitants of the region approximately two hundred years ago. Consequently, before embarking on this explorative journey, the researcher should become acquainted with the social nuances that shaped colonial Caribbean society, in order to develop an appreciation for the social component of genealogical research. This paper will focus on the factors that shaped Anglo-Caribbean culture by exploring those issues that existed in a highly stratified society, such as phenotype, social class, kinship, religion, and education. Biographical sketches are included which will provide further insight into those issues which affect family relationships, illustrate the social hierarchy created by categorization according to skin tone and social class, and provide greater insight and appreciation of the social issues which contributed to the formation of Anglo-Caribbean culture.

In order to be productive and successful, the researcher should seek answers to several burning questions: How was the society structured? What were the major religious denominations? What were the cultural norms and practices? What types of family structure existed and what were the prevailing social and economic conditions? These questions, along with those prompted by reading official records of birth, marriage, and death, will require the researcher to become acquainted with cultural and social issues which helped shape the society. These include kinship patterns, marriage practices, relationships in families and households, social customs, race and class structure, and general living conditions of the period under study. To support this process, knowledge of the legislation, occupations, educational opportunities, social statuses, and migratory patterns would provide a better understanding of the prevailing social climate, and ultimately lead to a more rewarding genealogical research experience.

Kinship and Family Structure

Kinship and marriage are regarded by social anthropologists as key components that determine how a society functions. Both foster harmonious relationships and encourage the establishment of functional alliances. Persons are recognized as kin when the line of descent can be traced directly from one to another (Kuper 1997, 190). Kinship establishes links between various groups of people and is regarded as the social tool that assists in the creation of customs and cultural practices as persons "cooperate with one another in an orderly social life" (Kuper 1997, 189).

The existence of both elementary and compound family structures in African society provides some insight into lineage, kinship, and family structures in Anglo-Caribbean society. Africans transported to the Caribbean brought their cultures and customs with them. The system of plantation slavery in the new world discouraged the establishment of the elementary family unit. Anthropologists acknowledge the existence of other family units such as the polygamous family unit; however, the traditional and compound family units are two structures prevalent among African societies. The traditional or elementary family unit is comprised of a father, mother, and their children and is regarded as the main unit in the kinship structure, while the compound family unit occurs when the male has children with two or more wives (Kuper 1997, 191). Higman (1975), in his paper on the slave family and households in the British West Indies, 1800–1834, argues that both cultural and economic circumstances contributed to the development of West Indian family structure. He supports the findings of eminent Caribbean historians and sociologists on the slave family structure; for example, Goveia's description of a slave family supports a widely held view on the Caribbean slave family:

> The slave family consisted effectively of the mother and her children who all belonged to the mother's owner though they might be born of different fathers. If a "husband" belonged to the same plantation, he could reside with his wife and their children, but in other circumstances it might be impossible for him to do so. In either case, it was the link with the mother which provided the basis for the existence of the slave family. The fact that the father was not even needed as a bread winner further reduced the importance of his role, and made it possible for the slave women to dispense completely with any form of stable union if they so desired. (Quoted in Higman 1975, 262)

The historical circumstances that shaped the lives of the peoples of the Caribbean are inextricably linked to race and social class. The establishment of the plantation system, and the introduction of African slaves as its labor, saw the evolution of a social structure that distinguished different groups. The family structure of the Afro-Caribbean family in the postemancipation era also differs from that of the traditional Eurocentric family unit of a male-headed, two-parent household with children all related to each other by blood or marriage. Some explanations include the survival of the African family structure, the institution of slavery, and the perpetuation of the plantation system, which discouraged the establishment of the elementary family unit. Michael G. Smith's analysis of the postemancipation Caribbean family structure illustrates this:

> In this region, family life is extremely unstable, marriage rates are low, especially during the earlier phases of adult life, and illegitimacy rates have always been high. Many households contain single individuals while others with female heads consist of women, their children and/or their grandchildren. The picture is further complicated by variations in the type and local distribution of alternative conjugal forms; and, characteristically, differing communities, social classes and ethnic groups institutionalize differing combinations of them. Excluding legal marriage, mating is brittle, diverse in form and consensual in base among these Creole or Negroid populations. (Quoted in Barrow 1996, 2)

Smith's observations echo the sentiments of other studies conducted on the Caribbean family. Most notably, his earlier work (Smith 1962) and that of Raymond T. Smith (1956) on the composition and structure of the Anglo-Caribbean family in the postemancipation era recognized the continuation of common-law unions and the predominance of female-headed households.[2] Smith (1962, 11) examines the difference between family structure and domestic organization and defines a household as "consisting of those persons who habitually share a common shelter and food." He further states that while a household may include cohabiting couples, it may not have an elementary family structure but more that of a compound family. Essentially, while households can be considered domestic units, they are not always domestic family units and can vary in kinship structure between the elementary family structure and the compound or extended family structure. For the genealogists familiar with tracing lineage through the male, the structure of a compound or matrilineal family presents something different. Smith describes the West Indies as a "culturally heterogeneous society which is subject to generalizations regarding family relations." The person considered the head of the household may not always be male but is seen as "the person whom the community as well as the household members regard as the head of the domestic group" (Smith 1962, 12, 15).

Raymond T. Smith, in his seminal work, *The Negro Family in British Guiana*, supports these views and goes further by examining the economic functions of the households and describing the activities undertaken by male- and female-headed households. In his analysis, he suggests that eleven different types of households can exist and provides a detailed discussion on their individual compositions and areas of overlap (Smith 1956, 75–78, 96–97).[3]

Given scholars' observations and the influence of slavery on family structure, the role of marriage versus common-law unions has generated much discussion. It is interesting that studies conducted on family life in Jamaica and Guyana showed that visiting, common-law unions, illegitimate births, and legal marriage occurred at all levels of society, regardless of race or class (Barrow 1996, 165). No matter the level, the children of these illegitimate unions invariably resided with their mother. In some instances, illegitimacy also signaled a common-law relationship in which the father of the child was from a higher class (Barrow 1996, 175). This structure and stratification of plantation society are succinctly captured in the following passage:

> By the late eighteenth century when the Caribbean slave society attained its highest stage of development, it has assumed a distinctive form. Masters and slaves, merchants and shippers, rulers and ruled, free and nonfree, white and nonwhite all constituted a closely integrated mutually interdependent grouping of distinct castes and classes. (Knight 1990, 121)

This social structure, along with its lines of delineation developed during plantation slavery, continued into the postemancipation colonial period. The economic and social benefits derived from slavery ensured that the planter class enjoyed dominance over the nonwhite population (Smith 1996, 143). Children, whether legitimate or illegitimate, were subject to a society in which the white culture was the dominant one and consequently defined social status (Barrow 1996, 177). The system of slavery and the dominance of the slave master over female slaves resulted in a hierarchical stratification of the population based on social class and color of skin. Skin tone became linked to social class, with persons with lighter complexions feeling socially superior to those with a darker skin tone. Categorization according to skin color continued into the postemancipation period and gave rise to a complex classification of skin tone based on the percentage of negro blood.[4] Smith (1988, 156, described in Barrow 1996, 178) provides a vivid description of societal structure:

> The turnover of white employees on sugar estates was remarkably high.... The life of the white staff was organized around the overseer's house and catered to by cooks, washers and cleaning servants provided by the estate, but it was customary for white men to form semi-permanent attachments to women—slave or free—who provided services beyond those laid down in the estate code.

The racial mixtures of offspring from relationships between the Creole population and individuals of the colonial administration were often captured in birth records (see, for example, Figure 1). Inclusion of these details in the official records is extremely useful for genealogists since it helps them to ascertain both the racial composition and social position of individuals.

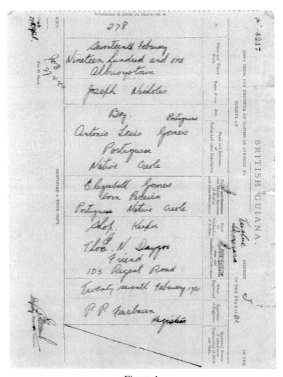

Figure 1

Religion and Education

Since slaves were considered property, slave owners were not required by law to record births and deaths of slaves. Consequently, researchers may need to consult plantation inventory records to ascertain whether the names of slaves were included among property holdings.[5] In the postemancipation period the church played a pivotal role in the religious and educational lives of the local population and their records provide vital genealogical information. Missions were established to convert the slaves in British Guiana and the London Missionary Society was one of the early ones. Many churches established schools and trained teachers (Rodney 1981, 114–15).

Tracing Lineage

Early census records provide details on households and often include information on race and occupation.[6] Colonial office reports give a level of detail on government operations that can be extremely useful. Early newspapers impart useful genealogical information, often listing the names of persons purchasing land and the sale and transfer of property. Details, including the name and race of persons entering and leaving the jurisdiction, are often included.[7] Newspaper notices and obituaries also provide fascinating detail on weddings and funerals.[8] Maps and early photographs should also be included in the search since they assist in the location of early settlements, plantations, and villages. Two biographical sketches are provided to illustrate actual experiences, kinship patterns, and social practices which occurred in Anglo-Caribbean colonial society.[9]

Biographical Sketch: Catherine Clementson

Born in 1874 in British Guiana, to a father who had migrated to Demerara from the island of Dominica and a Creole mother, she was raised in a coastal village. The second of three daughters, Catherine enjoyed a comfortable upbringing as her father was the village dispenser and her mother a nurse in the village hospital. She was of mixed race, her father being a mixture of Carib Indian and white and her mother colored, a mixture of negro and white. She was baptized in the Roman Catholic Church and attended the village primary school. At seventeen, Catherine was employed as a seamstress in the home of the plantation manager of an adjoining plantation. Originally from the island of Barbados, he was married and had three children. As a white employee of the colonial government, the manager was part of the colonial ruling class. Shortly after the death of his wife, the manager approached Catherine's parents and expressed his intention to start a relationship with her. They gave their consent and the manager made arrangements to purchase land and build a house in the village where Catherine's parents resided. It is interesting to note that one of the signatures on the manager's receipt for the land is Catherine's father. This suggests that Catherine may have been the unwilling subject of an arrangement sealed between two men. As a young woman in that era she was in no position to object. The wide age difference between Catherine and the manager also suggested that this relationship may not have been fully consensual. She was twenty-two when her first child was born and he, forty-nine. Oral accounts indicate that the manager never lived in the home he built but would visit often. Their union produced four children (see Figure 2). Although Catherine was unmarried and her children illegitimate, the complexion of her children gained them social acceptance and upward mobility. They attended secondary schools that did not enroll students of a dark complexion at that time. In contrast, her sister's offspring of a legal marriage were of a dark complexion and could not attend the same school. Catherine's relationship with the manager ended several years later and she began a relationship with a fellow villager. They married and lived in the house built for her by the manager, who eventually returned to Barbados after retiring from government service. Catherine lived her entire life in the same village until her death at the age of sixty-three. A newspaper clipping of her obituary in June 1938 indicates that her funeral was well attended. The house and land where she spent most of her life were inherited by Catherine's children and remained in their possession for almost fifty years before being sold.

Figure 2

Biographical Sketch: Murry Cummins

Murry Cummins was born a slave in Demerara, British Guiana around 1818. His exact date of birth remains sketchy since there were no official records for slaves. Based on his burial record, Murry Cummins was in his twenties at the time of the emancipation from slavery and his apprenticeship in 1838. Oral accounts indicate that he was a member of the Anglican Church and married with one child, a daughter. British colonial papers record that he resided at Plantation Non-Pareil on the east coast of Demerara. Murry was one of the original purchasers of Plantation New Orange Nassau, the second plantation purchased by former slaves in 1840, just six years after emancipation. Colonial records indicate that about 133 former slaves pooled their savings to purchase the plantation for $50,000. The records list the contribution made by each person to the purchase and the plantation where each purchaser resided. Murry Cummins contributed $250 towards the purchase of Plantation New Orange Nassau (British Parliamentary Papers 1841, 120). Shortly after it was bought, Murry moved with his wife and daughter to the newly purchased plantation, now renamed Buxton by its new owners. Unfortunately, he died at the young age of thirty-eight, just a few years after the establishment of Buxton Village. He was buried in the churchyard of St. Augustine Anglican Church at Buxton. Although illiterate, Murry left a will, dated August 26, 1950 and signed with an "X," in which his land and property are bequeathed to his daughter. Oral accounts indicate that his daughter, Martha, managed her father's property and appeared to be very active in village life. There is a street there named Cummins but it is unclear whether it is named after her or her father. Martha never married but had three daughters through different liaisons. One daughter married a sugar factory worker from Barbados. Their union produced six children. The land which Murry Cummins saved to purchase is now lost to his descendants.

Both biographies illustrate the socio-economic stratification and circumstances that existed at the time. They also illustrate the challenges that researchers will encounter when conducting family history research on the Anglo-Caribbean family. The critical roles played by gender, education, religious affiliation, and social status in society are evident. The existence of inter-island migration among British Caribbean colonies is captured along with the ethnic diversity of the migrants. While a dominant male presence in society is evident in both cases, the position of women ranges from one of subservience to that of main breadwinner and head of household. Catherine Clementon's life story illustrates the impact of the social conditions that existed in post-emancipation colonial society. Her life was shaped by race, gender, and social class. Although the manager was in a position to remarry, he chose instead to enter into a visiting relationship. The woman in the relationship appeared to have little control over her life and was subject to the will of her father and partner. Although her children were the result of an illegitimate union, their physical appearance qualified them for higher social acceptability. The family name or surname also played a critical role when tracing lineage. In the case of Catherine, her children assumed the name of their father, while Martha Cummins's children, also born out of wedlock, bore her surname.

The biographies also demonstrate the importance of orally transmitted family information in tracing lineage and kinship patterns. Often relayed anecdotally, the oral record is a useful source for acquiring essential information on family members, for often the first clues regarding family linkages, migration, and miscegenation are obtained through conversation. Murry Cummins's role as one of the original purchasers of Plantation New Orange Nassau was often recounted by his descendants but could only be verified once the colonial record of his name was found among other details. The entrepreneurial spirit of recently freed slaves is captured in the second biographical sketch and also serves to demonstrate their desire for economic independence within a rigid social structure.

Family structure and kinship linkages define all societies and are the foundation of genealogical exploration. Genealogy also relies on an understanding and appreciation of the social and economic circumstances of the period. Researchers often face a paucity of data or records, for many have been lost as a result of destruction from natural disasters, or social incidents such as riots and rebellions. Additionally, a tropical environment often hastens the deterioration of paper-based records. Preserving the history of our ancestors ensures that future generations understand the struggles their forebears encountered, and that they seek to develop a greater awareness of their lives. Ultimately, this will lead to a greater appreciation of identity and heritage, of who we are and where we have come from.

Undertaking genealogical research presents many challenges to both the seasoned as well as the novice researcher. Success depends on the existence of pertinent records but also on an understanding of the culture and society under study. The researcher also needs to adopt a critical and analytical approach to the task and to employ the technique of delving beyond and beneath written sources to discover hidden truths. Often frustrating, it demands the adoption of a methodical approach to research, an inordinate amount of patience, and an unwavering commitment to checking and rechecking records. However, after sources are verified, questions answered, and previously unknown records identified, this painstaking research evolves into an exercise that is both satisfying and rewarding.

NOTES

1. The countries of the Anglo-Caribbean are Anguilla, Antigua and Barbuda, The Bahamas, Barbados, Belize, British Virgin Islands, Dominica, Grenada, Guyana, Jamaica, St. Kitts, Nevis, Saint Lucia, St. Vincent and the Grenadines, Trinidad and Tobago, and Turks and Caicos.

2. See also Greenfield (1959) and Herskovits and Herskovits (1947).

3. The different households identified are married (legally), common-law married, single mother or single father, single (no children, never married), widower, widow, common-law widower, common-law widow, separated, common-law separated, divorced.

4. Distinctions in skin tone were based on the percentage of the mixture with negro ancestry. Terms used included Mulatto (one-half black ancestry), Quadroon (one-quarter black ancestry), Octoroon (one-eighth black ancestry), and Sambo (three-quarters black ancestry). See the Multiple Heritage Project's terminology list at http://www.mix-d.org/files/resources /Terminology_Chart_09.pdf

5. Demerara slave registers exist for the years 1817, 1820, 1823, 1826, and 1832. Slave registers also exist for several Anglo-Caribbean islands.

6. The Church census for Demerara was conducted c1830–1840, and records the names, ages and races of inhabitants in the colony.

7. Examples can be found in the *Essequibo and Demerary Royal Gazette*, 1815.

8. Births, marriages, and deaths are recorded in colonial newspapers. A popular newspaper in the 1800s was the *Colonist* of British Guiana.

9. Biographical sketches included in the paper are taken from genealogical research undertaken by the author on her maternal and paternal family line.

REFERENCES

Barrow, Christine. 1996. *Family in the Caribbean: Themes and Perspectives*. Kingston: Ian Randle Publications.

British Parliamentary Papers. 1841. *Papers Relative to the West Indies. 1841. British Guiana*. London: HMSO.

Greenfield, Sidney M. 1959. *Family Organization in Barbados*. New York: Columbia University.

Haley, Alex. 1978. *Roots*. London: Picador: Pan Books.

Herskovits, Melville J., and Frances S. Herskovitz. 1947. *Trinidad Village*. New York: A. A. Knopf.

Higman, Barry W. 1975. "The Slave Family and Household in the British West Indies, 1800–1834." *The Journal of Interdisciplinary History* 6, no. 2: 261–87.

Knight, Franklin W. 1990. *The Caribbean: The Genesis of a Fragmented Nationalism*. New York: Oxford University Press.

Kuper, Adam, ed. 1997. *The Social Anthropology of Radcliffe-Brown*. London: Routledge & Kegan Paul.

Pearsall, Judy, ed. 1998. *The New Oxford Dictionary of English*. Oxford: Clarendon House.

Pine, Leslie Gilbert. 2015. "Genealogy." In *Encylopaedia Britannica Online*. Chicago: Encyclopaedia Britannica. http://www.britannica.com/topic/genealogy.

Rodney, Walter. 1981. *A History of the Guyanese Working People, 1881–1905*. Baltimore: Johns Hopkins University Press.

Smith, Michael G. 1962. *West Indian Family Structure*. Seattle: University of Washington Press.

Smith, Raymond T. 1956. *The Negro Family in British Guiana: Family Structure and Social Status in the Villages.* London: Routledge & Kegan Paul.

————. 1988. *Kinship and Class in the West Indies: A Genealogical Study of Jamaica and Guyana.* Cambridge: University of Cambridge Press.

Winick, Charles. 1977. *Dictionary of Anthropology.* New Jersey: Littlefield, Adams.

3. Ordinary Images: Appreciating Photographs of Children in a Pictorial Archive

Claire-Lise Bénaud

In the Center for Southwest Research Pictorial Archive at the University of New Mexico, photographs of children appear in a broad range of collections. The photographs discussed in this paper are an unexceptional sample and many archives in historical societies and universities have similar collections. Because the photographs are not exceptional in any way, archivists and librarians take them for granted and, up till now, have overlooked their significance. A closer look at these ordinary images is thought-provoking.

Most pictures of children in the Pictorial Archive were not taken by artists—even though some have artistic value—but by studio photographers, documentary photographers, and regular people. The Pictorial Archive has countless photographs of children shown either alone or with their families. It also contains group portraits that usually fall into the categories of school photos, sports teams, theater or dance productions. In this paper, we will focus on studio photographs of children and their families from Mexico and New Mexico. The Mexican photographs come from studios in Mexico City, Durango, León, Veracruz, and some others that are unidentified. Many images are in the *carte-de-visite* format. The New Mexican images come mostly from two photographic studios, the Cobb Studio in Albuquerque and Schmidt Studio in Chloride. These photographs of Mexican and New Mexican children date from the same time period, the late nineteenth century to World War I.

When one looks at these photographs, several questions come to mind. What is the image about? Who was the photographer? How was he or she influenced by tradition and culture? The cardinal question is still discussed today by the public and in the media: Do photographs act as indisputable evidence of a real event? The realist versus constructivist viewpoints, especially for documentary photographs as we find them in the Pictorial Archive, offer a valid debate. Susan Sontag (1973, 86), in her seminal work *On Photography,* states that the history of photography can be recapitulated as the struggle between two different imperatives: beautification, which comes from the fine

Who Are We Really?: Latin American Family, Local and Micro-Regional Histories, and Their Impact on Understanding Ourselves. Papers of the Fifty-Ninth Annual Meeting of SALALM, 2014.

arts, and truth-telling, which comes from journalism. She argues that photographs "furnish evidence" even though the picture may distort reality (Sontag 1973, 5).

Other academics contend that photographs are constructions subject to the same discursive formations as any other medium and cannot be regarded as a trace of reality. Images of children have an added layer of complexity. Their photographs are taken by adults and often represent the adults' aspirations. We do not know how the children feel about being in the picture or having to pose for studio photographers. It is impossible to reconstruct feelings. Do pictures reflect children's real experiences, since they are taken by adults and the children are only subjects? It is not only the photograph that matters, but what's in the eye of the beholder. The same photograph may be understood differently today than it was a hundred years ago. Meanings and visual cues are understood and shared by a particular society within a particular time period.

Rather than artistic influences, we are more concerned here with the sociohistorical influences and values that the photographer might not have consciously brought into play but are nevertheless present. At first glance, it seems that parents are interested to have photographs of their children because they want to see and remember them as they really were. However, in the last two centuries, as is the case today, families want to present their children as charming and cute. The pictures of these children show us what we want childhood to be.

Historical Perspective

Before the Enlightenment, children were represented in paintings like small, imperfect adults. Jean-Jacques Rousseau's treatise, *Emile,* about education and child-rearing, completely changed this perception. Rousseau considered man a *bon sauvage,* a noble savage, meaning that youth is inherently good and innocent. The concept of the child was transformed from that of an inefficient but potentially worthy small adult to that of a new class of being— innocent, helpless, needing education, special clothing, and special attention (Hixson 1977, 10). When photography came along in 1839, society's representation of children reflected this understanding. The ideal of the Romantic Child simply changed medium, from paintings and illustrations to photographs.

Mexican Photographs

The Pictorial Archive has significant holdings of Latin American photography, especially from Mexico (Davidson 2004). Many of these Mexican collections contain scarce and unique works and are from well-known photographers and artists. Despite this rich corpus, the Pictorial Archive holds few items from run-of-the-mill Mexican photographic studios. The emphasis on rare materials, while fundamental to Special Collections, is a detriment to the type of images discussed here.

New Mexican Photographs

In the nineteenth century, women of the expanding middle class stayed home to take care of their children and had them photographed to exhibit motherhood, to show status, and to record significant events. Having studio photographs taken, which became the craze starting in the 1860s, became a necessary step for these families. In the Pictorial Archive, there is a vast trove of studio photographs. These are of children from middle class families, families who could take time off from their chores, had the inclination to dress up their children, could make an appointment, and take them to a studio. The rise of the middle class "created a market for pleasant, undemanding pictures to hang on living-room walls" (O'Neill 1996, 3). Going to the photographer's studio was not a casual appointment, but a ritual like others of motherhood, such as christening, baptism, and birthday celebrations. The photos proved that women graduated from the role of wife to that of mother, so they were framed for display at home and were sent to family members.

Families

In family photographs, children wore their Sunday best and posed stiffly. Unlike current family photographs, it was not always apparent that the parents appreciated and loved their children. The ways the parents were dressed clearly reflected their status in society. The women wore fancy hats and elaborate

Image 1. "Group Portrait," photograph, Cobb Memorial Photograph Collection (PICT 000-119-0350), Center for Southwest Research, University Libraries, University of New Mexico.

dresses, the men wore jackets, starched shirts, and watch fobs. Not a hair was out of place. While the parents often wore dark clothing, the children were dressed in white or light colors. Both boys and girls were well-scrubbed; wore lacy dresses and bows in their hair, on their shoes, and at the collar; had carefully combed hair, which was often curled for the event. Very young boys wore dresses as was customary at the time. There were no children from the lower classes represented in these studio portraits. Nobody smiled at the camera.

The roles of mothers and fathers were clearly defined when one looks at these photographs. Fathers were placed in a slightly more prominent position and mothers sat back, had their youngest child on their lap and were surrounded by their other children (see Image 1). Fathers did not hold their children but were portrayed as the protector or as the educator while mothers were portrayed as the nurturer with babe in arms. In many photographs, little girls emulated their mothers. They sat on chairs and crossed their legs, just as their mothers did, and held their baby sister or brother. Girls clearly fell in the domestic realm while boys often stood. This pictorial convention was true for family pictures as well as portraits of children photographed only with their mother or father.

Motherhood

Photographs of children with their mother far outnumber pictures of children with their father. In Image 2, the mother lovingly holds her little boy on

Image 2. "Mrs. Blanchard and Son," photograph, Cobb Memorial Photograph Collection (PICT 000-119-0342), Center for Southwest Research, University Libraries, University of New Mexico.

her lap, surrounding him with one arm and also holding his hand. However, her facial expression is quite stern and contrasts with her affectionate gesture. She wears a dressy dark gown with lace and a high collar. Her young son wears velvet knickerbockers, a velvet jacket, and a loose white shirt with a *lavaliere* or cravat. His hair is curled. The mother in Image 3 is portrayed in the same affectionate pose. While she does not hold her little girl on her lap, she makes up for it by having her face next to her child's as if she were about to kiss her. She smiles, a rare occurrence in photographs of the time, and also wears a dark dress with a white lace collar. Her young girl is dressed in a white outfit with a matching lacy bonnet. The children in these two photographs are rather stiff, appear obedient, and stare at the camera. These very common images give a good representation of motherhood in the late 1800s. The mothers are depicted as loving, usually more in their poses than their facial expressions, and their clothing as well as their children's indicate they come from good families. Such images intend to show that they are good and responsible mothers who love their well-scrubbed, docile children. When background and furniture are present in the images, these elements bring a sense of opulence. In Image 4, the chair is well-cushioned and fashionable with a large tassel hanging on the back, a very ornate table is visible on the side, and the background wall has moldings.

Image 3. "Mother and Child," photograph, Mexico Photograph Collection (PICT 991-020, box 1, cartes-de-visite, portraits—groups), Center for Southwest Research, University Libraries, University of New Mexico.

Image 4. "María Rodríguez de Alonso Holding Baby"
photograph, Mexico Photograph Collection (PICT 991-
020, box 1, portraits—Female—Identified), Center for
Southwest Research, University Libraries, University of
New Mexico.

Image 5. "Dr. Pearce and Daughter," photograph, Cobb
Memorial Photograph Collection (PICT 000-119-0346),
Center for Southwest Research, University Libraries,
University of New Mexico.

Fatherhood

In contrast, the father in Image 5 does not have his daughter on his lap. Instead, the little girl is standing on a chair and he holds her with a protective gesture. It is a controlling grip, as shown by the wrinkle on her dress, maybe because the child appears not to enjoy having her picture taken. The father does not express tenderness as the mothers did. The little girl wears a light-colored dress, a pinafore with a lacy top, and a ribbon in her ringleted hair. In these photographs of children with either their mother or father, the child is the central figure. The parents' bodies are not fully visible and only parts of their arms appear in the photos. There is no background and the viewer is not distracted by any other props such as furniture. In the few instances in which the father holds a baby and is surrounded by his other young children with no mother present in the image, can we deduce that the mother has died in her prime?

Babies

The baby photograph proves that a woman has achieved the rank of motherhood. There are numerous photographs of babies in christening gowns with lace and embroidery, and propped into position. This makes for awkward poses. The photo of the baby, though not the baby him- or herself who is hardly seen, makes a statement about the family's position and sociocultural status. The gown matters more than the child and emphasizes the event rather than the baby. These images do not reflect anything intimate or domestic. It is clear that the clothes make the person even at this tender age. These photos exemplify the rituals, especially baptism, surrounding the photographs during this era. Clearly baby worship and the adulation of the mother were complementary ideologies at the turn of the century in both Mexico and New Mexico (Gear 1987, 421). While portraits of babies were very formal in the 1870s, more informal ones were dominant by the 1890s through the end of World War I. Both types of photographs, formal and more informal, "used a basic format that studios used with little deviation over the decades" (Gear 1987, 423). In her article "The Baby's Picture: Woman as Image Maker in Small-Town America," Josephine Gear (1987, 433) contends that "all references to the external world, the family, or the home, have been expunged from these portraits, making the portrait space a timeless, immaterial one, a free zone for the projection of the mother's needs and feelings" (see Image 6).

In some instances, real objects creep into the photos. Children seem to be shown with their toys. While their clothing is only worn on the day the picture was taken, or a formal event, such as a baptism or going to church, their toys are "real." We can see children with rattles, hoops, toy horses, wheeled horse-and-carts, or dolls. However, if one takes a closer look, even the toys do not look worn-out and well-loved but fresh and unsoiled. Sometimes another real surrogate of a toy, such as a set of keys, is present in the picture, probably to

Image 6. "Lew Hearn's Baby," photograph, Henry A. Schmidt Pictorial Collection (PICT 000-179-0004), Center for Southwest Research, University Libraries, University of New Mexico.

Image 7. "Margueritta and Mesa Rose" photograph, Cobb Memorial Photograph Collection (PICT 000-119-0329), Center for Southwest Research, University Libraries, University of New Mexico.

distract the child while the picture was taken. The puppy is also a great favorite and functions as a surrogate for the stuffed animal, but with an extra cuteness factor (see Image 7).

Children

Photographs of children, like those of babies, appear in serene and still spaces, and reflect the ideal of the Romantic Child. These portraits are not intimate or domestic and do not reflect tensions and strains inherent in childhood. In Image 8, a little girl stands next to a table draped with a dark cloth. Her light-colored outfit contrasts with the dark fabric on the table and consists of a lacy dress, white socks and shoes. She wears what looks like a crown on her head with a veil flowing down her back. She looks like a very young bride, feminine and innocent. A basket of flowers on the table brings a bit of nature, though very tame, and reinforces the romanticism of the image. This type of image is very sentimental and even soppy. In Image 9, two children are seated in a pose that today would suggest a photograph of adults. The little

Image 8. "Girl with Veil," photograph, Mexico Photograph Collection (PICT 991-020, box 1, cartes-de-visite, portraits—children), Center for Southwest Research, University Libraries, University of New Mexico.

Image 9. "John and Merl Blinn," photograph, Henry
A. Schmidt Pictorial Collection (PICT 000-179-0401),
Center for Southwest Research, University Libraries,
University of New Mexico.

girl rests her head on the boy's shoulder, she is very pretty, rosy-cheeked, has
curly long hair, wears a light colored ruffled dress, and has a dreamy gaze. The
little boy wears a suit and looks ahead. There is a mildly romantic subtext.
Even though the two children are brother and sister, their parents could project
what they would become. The little sister suggests the role of the wife that she
would be one day, devoted to her husband, her older brother, already dressed
as a man, steering the couple towards a happy future. Children wear their best
clothing in these photographs, nothing dirty or torn, and some wear costumes
to further enhance this ideal. Girls wear white puffy dresses to increase their
femininity and girlishness, and proclaim their ethereal purity. Boys wear sailor
suits or jackets and ruffled shirts. For older children, toys have been replaced
with objects that indicate their future selves. A boy smokes a cigar and another
holds a pocket watch, telling the viewer what powerful men they will become;
a girl holds a fan, indicating that one day she will be a society woman. Parents
can project what their children will become as adults but reality sometimes
intrudes in the photographs. In some instances, boys wear formal suits but
tired boots which contrast with their pristine outfits. The boots look a bit
scruffy since it may have been more difficult for parents to fully control how
clean their children's shoes were.

Backdrops and Props

The backdrop of the studio enhances the imaginary world: serene, nostalgic, innocent, and idealized. In the Pictorial Archive, two types of backdrops dominate: the outdoors, an idyllic rural world, and the indoors, the interior of an affluent home. For predominantly urban audiences, quaint rural backdrops represent the nostalgia for a vanishing agrarian world (Higonnet 1998, 51). In New Mexican photographs, outdoor backdrops show flowering bushes and ferns with lush grass on the floor to represent the ground. This type of countryside does not exist anywhere in New Mexico, making it even more surreal. Some backdrops also include a white picket fence opening into what looks like the Garden of Eden, as if the child were about to enter a heavenly space. In the Mexican photographs, rural backdrops are similar, representing lush vegetation. In several photographs, there are mixed elements: the backdrop represents the outdoors but the floor is covered by a rug.

To make these photographs even more enticing, some children are dressed as country folk, reminiscent of Marie Antoinette dressing as a shepherdess a century earlier. In Image 10 a girl sleeps, holding a broad-brimmed straw hat, next to a basket of flowers. The floor is littered with straw. The girl depicted is not a country girl. While she is barefoot, her feet and pinafore are clean and she shows no sign of ever having worked in the fields. She is the archetype

Image 10. "Amy Schmidt," photograph, Henry A. Schmidt Pictorial Collection (PICT 000-179-0095), Center for Southwest Research, University Libraries, University of New Mexico.

of the sleeping beauty. Image 11 shows two dark-skinned girls, one standing and the other sitting. They may be indigenous. They are barefoot and dressed in identical and very plain clothing. Each wears a pristine white dress with an immaculate piece of plain white cloth around her shoulders. They are dressed as country girls, the stereotypical dress you would expect, but their clothing looks more like a costume than real and their feet are unsoiled. They look primeval. In contrast, the backdrop represents a lush garden with a balustrade with several potted plants, suggesting a patio or a balcony of a mansion. In both images, the young girls look virginal, innocent, and are surrounded by an imaginary garden. Even though real children often worked in the fields or at home, none of these photographs reflect this fact.

Children with pets enhance the bucolic backdrop and show that they are close to nature. In the archive, several children are accompanied by dogs, often very large, such as springer spaniels or retrievers. In the case of children accompanied by absurdly large dogs, it cues the "viewer's projection of his or her adult self into the image as the child's protector" (Higonnet 1998, 34). Boys are seen with dogs while girls, more often, with puppies, the harmless version of dogs.

The other prevalent backdrop shows the interior of a home, refined and prosperous. One backdrop shows the foyer of an opulent home, featuring a

Image 11. "Two Girls in Studio," photograph, Mexico: Selected 20th Century Photograph Collection (PICT 998-021, box 1), Center for Southwest Research, University Libraries, University of New Mexico.

grand staircase on one side with an ornamental lamp standing on top of the finial, and a marble fireplace with an elaborate mantelpiece on the other. A painting hangs on the wall. There is wainscoting in the back and the ceiling is decorated with a garland frieze. In other instances, urban sophistication is created by props such as fine furniture, carved tables, rich velvety fabrics, wrought-iron staircases, columns, fireplaces, and fake flowers. This is particularly true of Mexican *cartes-de-visite*, small photographs that began to be exchanged like calling cards in the 1850s, which employ more props than backdrops. In several photographs, children stand on chairs or stools, either to make them look bigger or because they are dwarfed by the backdrop or the props and need to be heightened.

In some instances, the studio is set up in an effort to reflect a traditional activity of children: play. In one example, children act as if playing hide-and-seek. The whole effect is stilted and does not convey the fun of the game. In other instances, a boy poses as if playing the violin and a little girl holds up her dress, revealing a lacy petticoat, as if dancing. Does the boy know how to play the violin or does the violin show that his family had an appreciation of the finer things? Similarly, in Image 12, a young girl stands and rests her arm on a table covered with a flowery cloth. A book is on the table. She wears a dark dress with short puff sleeves, has a low décolletage, and her lacy pantalets

Image 12. "Girl with Fan," photograph, Mexico Photograph Collection (PICT 991-020, box 1, cartes-de-visite, portraits—children), Center for Southwest Research, University Libraries, University of New Mexico.

show above her stockings and high boots. Her waist is cinched by a wide belt. She is bejeweled—earrings, a bracelet, and a necklace—and holds a fan in her hands. Her outfit proclaims that she belongs to a well-off family and the book signals that she is educated. Like clothing, backdrops and props enable parents to project that their children will be wealthy, refined, and well-educated in the future.

Conclusion

These pictures of children, taken at the turn of the century by studio photographers, provide visual clues to the Mexican and New Mexican societies of the era. The conventions are similar and there are no noticeable differences in portraits, except for the carte-de-visite format in Mexico. Neither place is well represented either in its landscape or its people. Most of the children are from middle- or upper-class families, a small minority in Mexico and New Mexico. Instead, the Romantic Child, a construction which originated in Europe, is the prevalent image. Childhood innocence is the predominant message. Going to the photographic studio is a social rite and these photographs demonstrate the social values of the time. Children are depicted as obedient, cute, and impeccably dressed; motherhood is glorified; fathers are pictured more prominently in group settings but never as caregivers; and through *mise-en-scène*, thus carefully arranged, parents try to project a future for their children.

Photographers today, both professional and amateur, still try to capture the innocence of childhood. The serious faces of the past have been replaced with the obligatory smile. This does not mean that photographs of children are any more "natural" than in the past. Photographs are still socially constructed to present childhood untainted by life's vicissitudes and show children experiencing "an unmediated life of pure feeling, honest, guilt free, fun loving, candid, spontaneous, and direct" (Hixson 1997, 10). The role created by both society at large and families functions as in the past. We still romanticize childhood and some representations are absent: battered children, the plight of the homeless, and other types of violence. At the turn of the twenty-first century, pictures of children are still one of the most common, the most sacred, and the most cherished of images. However, we are living through a major change in our culture's understanding of childhood. Society has recognized child abuse, and pictures of children have become some of the most controversial images of our time (Higonnet 1998, 7). Nonetheless, photographs of children in archives continue to gloss over difficulties and erase conflict just as it is treated in society at large.

REFERENCES

Davidson, Russ. 2004. *Latin American Holdings in the University of New Mexico Library: An Illustrated History and Guide*. Albuquerque: UNM University Libraries.

Gear, Josephine. 1987. "The Baby's Picture: Woman as Image Maker in Small-Town America." *Feminist Studies* 13: 419–42.

Higonnet, Anne. 1998. *Pictures of Innocence: The History and Crisis of Ideal Childhood*. London: Thames and Hudson.

Hixson, Kathryn. 1997. "Youthful Hysteria and Wild-Eyed Delirium: Youth Culture Fights Back." In *Presumed Innocence*, curated by Jean Crutchfield, 10–17. Richmond: Anderson Gallery, Virginia Commonwealth University and Seattle: University of Washington Press.

O'Neill, Richard. 1996. *The Art of Victorian Childhood*. New York: Smithmark.

Sontag, Susan. 1973. *On Photography*. New York: Farrar, Straus and Giroux.

4. Discovering Oneself through Ancestors' Diaries

John B. Wright

I was raised hearing stories of my ancestors. As a little boy, I was particularly intrigued and scared by those my Grandma Jake, Ada Robinson Jacobson, told of her grandfather, James Oliverson. I remember her sharing the memory of her only contact with Grandpa Oliverson, of an incident which occurred when she was two or three years old. By that time a widower, Grandpa Oliverson came for dinner at her family's home. He expected to eat when the family sat down to dinner. He did not want to hear the whining, bickering, or even giggling of children when it was time to eat. When this commotion occurred he raised his strong hand, pounded the table and loudly declared: "Danna bust to it!" As mealtime progressed, the children once again began horsing around, tickling each other, and laughing. Grandpa Oliverson warned with his words: "If you laugh at the table, you'll cry before you go to bed."

When my Grandma told me this story I was intrigued because I thought it was rather funny that he would say such things. I remember being scared because I thought that I would not have wanted to eat dinner with him. I often wondered why a person would cry before going to bed if he or she laughed at the table. This memory of my Grandma's always made me feel that perhaps her Grandpa Oliverson was a mean man. Then I saw his photograph!

Figure 1. James Oliverson

Who Are We Really?: Latin American Family, Local and Micro-Regional Histories, and Their Impact on Understanding Ourselves. Papers of the Fifty-Ninth Annual Meeting of SALALM, 2014.

When I first saw this picture as a child, I was quite certain that he was mean. I was raised in a family and religious culture that valued ancestors so I was familiar with their pictures. By the time I became a teenager, I could recognize all of the pictures we had of our ancestors. I could also recite the names of my grandparents, great grandparents, and even most of my great, great grandparents. I knew how they were related to me.

Here is how I'm connected to James Oliverson:

John Wright (me)
Marvada Jacobson Wright (mother)
Ada Robinson Jacobson (grandmother)
Matilda Oliverson Robinson (great grandmother)
James Oliverson (great, great grandfather)

In addition to these names, I could give basic information about other family lines. I knew a lot of their birthdates, where they were born, and some of their family members but that's about it. Every one of my direct ancestors older than grandparents were already gone so I never knew them personally, only their names on a page, a few facts about each one, some stories about them, and perhaps a picture. That all changed in 1992 when I was able to transcribe James Oliverson's diaries.

Grandma Jake had two volumes. The first contained entries from 1884 through 1886 and the second, 1886 through 1888. I found it interesting that Oliverson made entries for almost every day during these four years and I supposed there must be other diaries available. After a process of investigating, searching, and finding that would take too long to describe here, I learned of ten other volumes. Over several months, I acquired copies of these ten and transcribed all of them along with the two volumes owned by Grandma Jake. When completed, I had a compilation of his diaries running from 1852 through 1893, referred to collectively throughout the rest of this paper as the *Diary*. There are some sizeable gaps in the *Diary*, largely because I have not been able to find any other volumes, but this was quite a wonderful find for my family and me.[1]

Diaries, journals, letters, and memoirs are examples of important sources for the historian and are commonly understood to be personal documents.

The diary has been called "the personal document *par excellence*." What is special about diaries is that they are written for strictly personal use and at the same time as the events described take place.... The fact that the diary records the writer's actions, opinions, feelings and points of view at that specific moment in time makes this type of document a precious and unique testimony to the individual's inner life (as well as providing a precise description of the unfolding of the events in which he is involved). (Corbetta 2003, 290)

While transcribing the *Diary*, I quickly became aware of the fact that Oliverson persistently wrote in it almost every day of his life. Though his spelling was not very consistent, he read a lot and tried to educate himself on various subjects. He immigrated to the United States from England as a young man. He migrated west in 1852, eventually settling in Kaysville, Utah. In 1860, he and his family moved north into Cache Valley with several other families to establish a new town that eventually became known as Franklin, Idaho. He lived in Franklin but spent several years working in a lumberyard in Dillon, Montana. He spent substantial periods of time away from his family to provide for them and wrote many letters home to them. He traveled by train often, which was certainly his preferred mode of transportation. I learned that he had a lot of respect for his adopted country and always mentioned the celebrations that occurred on July 4. He also was happy to report each March 3 that he had a birthday, as did his son, Levi, who shared that birthday. He reported briefly on events that happened in the town: the weather, work he performed, business transactions he made, trips to visit family, letters he sent and received. I came to know what topics would cause him to become agitated. He certainly was an independent, liberal-minded man. He valued the ability to be free in his new country, enjoyed the opportunities available to him, and liked making something of himself and his property. He defended his right to make his own decisions and did not appreciate anyone trying to take that privilege away from him. He was detail-oriented and kept track of both money he owed and money owed to him.

While diaries are valuable historical sources, they often have limitations. They are great sources to learn of events that occurred and what the diarist thought of those events. Consequently, however, diaries cannot fully help us contextualize and completely understand history. Through them we learn how one person perceived the world around him, but they often do not provide enough context for that perception. Diaries cannot help us completely understand events because they only offer one point of view. However, the great benefit of diaries as historical documents is their contemporary nature, and that they mention events that we can investigate further. As Pimlott puts it:

> Diaries tell the truth, the partial truth, and a lot more beside the truth....In them, you seek—and often find—an atmosphere, a sense of mood of the moment, which could not be acquired in any other way. They should never, ever, be taken as the last word. But as raw material for reconstruction of the past they are as invaluable as they are savagely entertaining. (2002, 2–3)

Let us consider the strengths and limitations of using diaries as a historical resource by considering entries from Oliverson's *Diary*. In transcribing the *Diary* entries below, I have retained spelling and punctuation as found. When I felt it necessary to add missing letters, words, or phrases that would help the reader better understand what was written, I have added those in square brackets. However, for this article, I am changing the font to illustrate the common occurrence in Oliverson's *Diary* entries to record an *event*, recorded in *italics*, and a **response** in **bold**, which is usually an emotional one. There are two entries that I want to use to demonstrate this point, regarding Oliverson's involvement with: 1) the *Mormon Tribune*[2] and 2) a free school administered by the Presbyterians. I think both will prove interesting for librarians because one relates to a publication while the other relates to education. We will consider one at a time.

Entry 1: Oliverson's Involvement with the *Mormon Tribune*

May 30th Munday [1870] Been at work on cub river water Ditch to day been cold and cloudy All day the river is riseing fast Storming in the mountains grasshopers very bad in Utah Valley Bishop Hatch and the Teachers cut of[f] 3 men yesterday For takeing and reading the Mormon Tribune **free Utah Bah!!!**

From this entry, we learn of an event that had taken place on the previous day, Sunday, May 29, 1870: "*Bishop Hatch and the Teachers cut of[f] 3 men yesterday For takeing and reading the Mormon Tribune.*" We also learn Oliverson's response to the event: "**free Utah Bah!!!**" However, we don't have any context with which to understand the event or adequately evaluate the appropriateness of his response. Let us try putting the May 30, 1870 entry in context with others that address the same topic. That should help us better understand both the event recorded in Entry 1, and Oliverson's response to it. A previous entry is:

May 29th Sunday [1870] At home all day reading I whent On the acre Lots to see how the Wheat Looked very Cloudy all day And cold 15 chickens Hatchd Out today Blowing hard from They South this afternoon

Subsequent entries are:

Sunday ~~Saterday~~ June 5th [1870] Whent to meeting this morning They cut the 3 men off From the church that was up Before the Teachers Last Sunday For contemped of preasthood Last Sunday the aledge fault was Subscribing for the mormon Tribune and reading of the same **But in realalty for being free to think for themselves and not Leting some other man think For them**

Wednesday June 15th [1870] I sold to Joseph Stone this morning 1 Acre Lot for 3 Bushells of wheat 1 old plough for 2 bits I receved on subscribing for the Mormon Tribune No. 24 this morning very strong wind from south West to day

Friday June 17th [1870] made 2 pair of posts this morning and Put 2 pannels of fence up in front of Lot Threatened for subscribing for the Mormon Tribune with dire purcutions ~~in~~ from the people of franklin **Some of them very warm** *to day some of the teams who whent from hear to montania with fr[e]ight Has got back this morning*

Munday June 20th [1870] grate preparation Being made to receve Brigham
young all out dresst up The company is Expected between 4 and 5 o.clock
the[y] arrived a Little Before 4 o.clock and held meeting in the meeting house[3]

These additional entries help us understand the event and Oliverson's response. We learn immediately from the entry for Sunday, May 29, 1870, that he did not attend the church meeting where the event took place. So, he recorded the event the next day, after the fact. Did he learn about it from his family members or friends who had attended the meeting? We do not know. We also learn that Oliverson had an interest in going to the church meeting the next Sunday, June 5, because he attended and then reported on it that day instead of doing other work or reading as he had the week before. In fact, the meeting attended was the only thing he mentions for the June 5 entry. Perhaps he was interested to learn more about the event and become better informed on what occurred. In the entry, Oliverson shared what he learned. We learn that three men were cut off from the church for the charge of contempt of priesthood. They allegedly demonstrated that contempt by subscribing to the *Mormon Tribune*. We also learn more about how Oliverson responded to the event of May 29. He stated that, in his opinion, the real fault was that these three men were willing to think for themselves and not allow some other man to think for them.

We do not learn the identity of these three men, nor do we learn of the "Teachers" who decided to excommunicate them. We are left to assume, however, that it was the "Teachers" who did it, and maybe not Bishop Hatch, as he was mentioned in the May 30 entry but not in the second rendering of the event as recorded on June 5. We would need to further investigate official Church records to know these facts. However, we do learn from subsequent June 15 and June 17 entries, that Oliverson stated his feelings about this event, because he received the *Mormon Tribune* No. 24 and then was threatened by townspeople for subscribing to and receiving the next issue of the weekly newspaper. Was this an attempt by Oliverson to demonstrate that he also thought for himself? And what of the *Mormon Tribune*? What was it? Why did subscribing to such a paper cause such a reaction by Church officials?

In order to provide more contextualization for Oliverson's Entry 1, I provide a brief history of that newspaper. The *Mormon Tribune* was first published on January 1, 1870. Its predecessor, *The Utah Magazine*, was a new periodical that made its debut in Salt Lake City in January 1868. It attempted to promote the ideas of its editors and publishers, E. L. T. Harrison, Edward W. Tullidge and William S. Godbe, and served as the official voice of their New Movement. The New Movement wanted to break open the closed economic and political systems of the region and loosen or eliminate what was perceived as the exclusive control of Brigham Young in both these areas of concern. The Mormon Church, upon its arrival in the Salt Lake Valley two decades earlier, had pursued an economy based on agriculture and home industry. With the impending transcontinental railroad, which was completed in May 1869 at Promontory Summit in Utah, the Church established a network of cooperative stores. They were known as Zion's Cooperative Mercantile Institution (ZCMI) and were set up in order to safeguard the interests of the Zion community and its economy. Members of the Church were expected to conduct all buying and selling of merchandise at the cooperative stores. One result of their continual antagonism toward the Church through their newspaper was the eventual excommunication of Godbe, Harrison, and Tullidge.

In January 1870, *The Utah Magazine* became a weekly called *Mormon Tribune*. The new weekly openly challenged what its editors and publishers believed was Brigham Young's reliance upon the previously mentioned, antiquated economic system based on agriculture and home industry. They called to open up the economic policies of the region, in order to take advantage of mining interests and align its economy with that of the United States. By June 1870, Godbe, Harrison, and Tullidge agreed that retaining "Mormon" in the title might stifle the interest of other residents in their newspaper. So, they changed it to *The Salt Lake Daily Tribune and Utah Mining Gazette* which, by 1871, was again changed simply to *The Salt Lake Tribune*. It became an anti-Mormon newspaper and directly challenged the Church and its societal, political, and economic controls, which were often communicated in the Church-sponsored *Deseret News*. *The Salt Lake Tribune,* which is still published today, no longer is considered an anti-Mormon newspaper.

When the intentions of *The Utah Magazine* first became apparent, the *Deseret News*, which was at first very supportive of the new periodical, published a statement in its October 26, 1869 issue:

> *The Utah Magazine* is a periodical that in its spirit and teachings is directly opposed to the work of God. Instead of building up Zion and uniting the people, its teachings, if carried out, would destroy Zion, divide the people asunder, and drive the Holy Priesthood from the earth. Therefore, we say to our Brethren and Sisters in every place, *The Utah Magazine* is not a periodical suitable for circulation among or perusal by them and should not be sustained by Latter-day Saints. We hope this will be sufficient without ever having to refer to it again. (Malmquist 1971, 11)

No similar statement has been found with regards to the *Mormon Tribune*, but the 1869 statement above regarding the *The Utah Magazine* must have been the sentiment in 1870 with its successor. The leaders of the Church in Franklin, Idaho, believed that the ideas and principles touted by the *Mormon Tribune* were detrimental to maintaining their Mormon community, so they consequently excommunicated the three men. It is clear from what is recorded in his *Diary* that Oliverson wanted to state that he supported the Franklin freethinkers, who read the *Mormon Tribune* and made their own decisions. He was willing to go on record as one of their supporters, even if the threats by local residents were quite heated.

There is no *Diary* entry which documents the event or Oliverson's response to it, because the time frame falls during one of the gaps mentioned earlier in this paper. However, Oliverson himself was excommunicated from the Church of Jesus Christ of Latter-day Saints on March 8, 1878. The family story is that he purchased yardage material or a shawl to give to his wife, from a traveling salesman instead of the ZCMI in Franklin, even though the cooperative had the same or a similar item in stock. As a member of the Church, Oliverson was expected to make purchases at the cooperative store but chose to buy the item from the traveling salesman because he got a better price. He soon found himself called before the local Church leaders on a Sunday and was excommunicated. Oliverson still continued to live in the town of Franklin, became its postmaster in 1888, and apparently was well respected. However, having felt that he was treated unjustly, he never reconciled with the Church, which explains why, after 1878, Oliverson wrote in his *Diary* as if he were an outside observer thereof. Let us consider one more entry to illustrate the important role his *Diary* plays as a historic document.

Entry 2: Oliverson's Involvement with a Free School Administered by the Presbyterians

> *Jan 17th Monday [1881] Another very fine morning The Mormans in church yesterday told the people that let their children go to the free school in this place taught by the Prepatairns would be cut off from the Morman church if the parents failed to take there children out right away* **O Lord keep me from such dogmatic teachings and away with such ignorance Such men that preach such doctrines and believes in the same ought to be away from children. Has their faith and doctrine going back to the dark ages as fast as time will take them**

From this entry, we learn of an event that took place on the previous day, Sunday, January 17, 1881 and Oliverson's response to the event. However, once again we lack any context for understanding the event or adequately evaluating the appropriateness of Oliverson's response. Let us try putting the January 17, 1881, entry in context with others that address the free school specifically, and education in general. These should help us better understand both the event recorded in Entry 2 and Oliverson's response to it. Because of the number of *Diary* entries to consider in this example, instead of quoting them entirely, I will include only their dates, those statements about the school, and Oliverson's responses.

Previous entries are:

> *Munday [January] 6th [1879]....Janett James and Levi commenced going to School today*[4]

> *March 3rd munday [1879]....Mr Meachams school Discontinued for the present time on cause sickness*

Oct. 15th Wednesday [1879]...I paid Jas. Packer Sen my School bill for 3 Sch [illegible]

Dec 12th Friday [1879]...had a visit From the School teacher

Dec 13th Saterday [1879]...Hauld a big Load of fire wood too the School to day

Dec 28th Sunday [1879]...The Children all went To Sunday School to Day after wich some Of them went to meeting

Jan 22nd Thursday [1880]...Left 2.00 dollors On School Bill

Feb 8th Sunday [1880]...Children all going to school

April 8th Thursday [1880]...Till and John Each had A pair of Shoes given Them By there School Teacher Mrs. Martian [Martin][5]

May 20th Thursday [1880]...I sent home By Thos. Holden Last Sunday 40.dollors 20 for T. Smart 10 for School Teacher and 10 For my wife

June 30th Wednesday [1880]...the people subscribed For a School house

Dec. 26th Sunday [1880] Christmas went off very quite I went to the [illegible] in the evening They had a very nice tree loaded with presents for the children who attented their school

Jan 5th Wednesday [1881]...The children commenced going to school today

Jan 9th Sunday [1881]...some of the children went to Sunday School

Jan 12th Wednesday [1881]...Had a note from Miss Nobles the school teacher about James staying out of school She wished me to see James about it **she seems very anxious about her scholars and I believe she has a great interest in learning them I corrected James about his conduct and wished him to apologized to Miss Nobles and ask her forgiveness and that he would not do it any more I hope he will do it**[6]

Jan 16th Sunday [1881] Very fine morning Sun shining bright and clear Looks fine this morning changed for the better The prospect for fine weather is good I fixed up the fence the same stock was in again last night

Subsequent entries are:

Jan 19th Wednesday [1881]...Had a note from the school teacher about the boys bad conduct at school **it greaves me very much if they do not do better I hope they will observe the rules of the school**

Feb 6th Sunday [1881]...The children have gone to Sunday School

Feb 9th Wednesday [1881]...John broke a window light at the school this afternoon

Feb 12th Saterday [1881]...James Levi and Tilly are doing very well trying to write

Feb 17th Thursday [1881]...Had a letter from Bear Lake to day and one from the school mistress about James bad conduct

Mar 1st Tuesday [1881]...James got the horses and we loaded a load of wood for the school house and took it down

Jan 6th Thursday [1887]...Our School commenced yesterday

March 8th Tuesday [1887]...our Boys all Turnd out of School **the Teacher has become very much against them has I have opposed her teaching So She is takeing it out Of the Boys**

March 9th Wednesday [1887]...I had to take Our Boys out of School in concequence of brutal Treatment of the teacher A Marian Kelly[7]

April 25th Wednesday [1888]...some boys Broke in the Public School Houes and committed Other Damage in Different parts Of town Brakeing fences Down

Feb 18th 1890 Tuesday...the Little boys Christopher and Will been Home from School The teacher told them to Stay home whilst we Had Sickness at Home[8]

Jan 25th Munday [1892]...Chris began Going to School this Morning

Feb 1st Munday [1892]...chris Started to go to School to day he has been Sick this Last week

August 7th Sunday [1892]...the boys gone to Sunday school

Nov 20th Sunday [1892] the boys gone to Sunday School

Nov 28th Munday [1892]...Chris and Richard commenced going to school this morning[9]

As in the already examined Entry 1, Oliverson was not in church to witness the event described in Entry 2. We learn that on Sunday, January 16, 1881, he was out repairing a fence that had allowed animals to reenter his field. The weather that day was sunny and very promising. This stands in contrast to what happened in church on January 17, 1881. We witness once again that Church leaders used the threat of excommunication to rein in their members who seemed, from their perspective, to be a little out of control. We obtain names of teachers: Mr. Meachum and Miss Nobles. We discover that Oliverson mentioned his children in connection with the entries related to the school and/or education. We determine that he had some responsibility to pay fees and/or provide supplies for the school; e.g., the ten dollars he sent to the teacher and the load of firewood he hauled to the school. The other entries also tell us of the existence of a Sunday school. We have more information but not enough to help us contextualize the event recorded on January 17, 1881, nor determine the appropriateness of Oliverson's response to the event. In order to understand more about the school situation in Franklin, Idaho, we need to look elsewhere.

In *The History of a Valley: Cache Valley, Utah-Idaho*, J. Duncan Brite (1956) writes two chapters entitled "Non-Mormon Schools and Churches" and "The Public Schools," which give a brief history of education and schools in the Cache Valley area. The chapters also help us understand the plight of public education in the area and how non-Mormon schools and churches helped to fill that void. He describes in some detail the history of education and the roles played by the Episcopalians, Methodists, and Presbyterians in establishing schools and providing education for the children of Cache Valley. Education in the area was elementary. Many people, including adults, could not write, read, spell, or work with large numbers. The first school in Franklin and all of Idaho was taught by Hannah Comish in her home on the east side of the fort in the 1860s. (Brite 1956b, 343). "The early schools in Cache Valley were private schools conducted in homes or church, or were community schools conducted in log buildings built by the citizens. Tuition, if paid at all, was paid in money or in produce" (Brite 1956b, 321–22). By 1880, of the 4,022 children under the age of eighteen, only 2,389 were actually enrolled and only 41 percent of those attended. The budget was $9,000 and teachers averaged less than $250 a year in salary (Brite 1956b, 325). The early district schools were not free. Students paid anywhere from $0.60 to $1.50 per term and churches and schools worked hand in hand in the same buildings. It was often a challenge to educate all children as many were needed to work the fields and do other tasks (Brite 1956b, 321). While there were several non-Mormon churches involved in providing education for the area, I will focus on the role played by the Presbyterian Church as it sponsored the free school mentioned in Oliverson's diaries. In Brite's chapters we read that:

> Presbyterian mission schools were established in Utah before Presbyterian churches. By action of the general assembly of the Presbyterian Church, schools were largely supported through the Women's Board of Home Missions, and the teachers in them were women. Schools were to be established only where the people could not be reached by churches and where public schools were not likely soon to be set up [...]

> Between 1875 and 1879 eleven schools with eight hundred day pupils were established in Utah. Duncan J. McMillan, district missionary for the whole Mormon territory, had in mind an academy in the major town in each valley, surrounded with primary schools in the surrounding villages. Schools would be located around Logan: at Millville, Hyrum, Wellsville, Mendon, Smithfield, and Richmond in Utah, and in the Idaho area at Franklin, Malad, Samaria, Montepelier, and Paris. Over thirty six schools and six academies were contemplated. (1956a, 308–9)

Funds that covered about a fourth of the cost of these efforts were raised in the area served by the mission school. The largest donor was the Women's Board of Home Missions. It is estimated that the Presbyterians spent well over $1.5 million on education between 1875 and 1915. Presbyterian mission schools reached their height of activity in the early 1890s and began to decline as public schools took over (Brite 1956a, 311–14).

George K. Davies's *A History of the Presbyterian Church in Utah* states that "while other Protestant denominations were likewise at work in Utah, the Presbyterian Church characteristically and specifically worked its missionary program in the Mormon villages, towns, and cities." He also reports that in Utah "the school with the school teacher was first to be established, for the early workers were convinced that the vantage point of attack on Mormonism was through education. [...] After the school, there came the chapel and the church" (Davies 1945–1947).

Davies also includes descriptions of encounters between Presbyterian teachers, missionaries, preachers, and Mormons in various towns throughout the area, from southern Idaho to St. George in southern Utah. Some accounts are exaggerated while others are downplayed. It was common for Mormon Church leaders to strongly discourage their members from allowing their children to attend these schools. Some, like Oliverson and other folks in Franklin, Idaho, were even threatened with excommunication if they did allow it. Some Presbyterians felt, and undoubtedly were, threatened, intimidated, and snubbed while living in Mormon communities.

R. Douglas Brackenridge recounts some of these same stories, that Church leaders exhorted members to not permit or withdraw their children from attending the Presbyterian schools, sometimes accompanied by the threat of excommunication. He also retells the feelings of harassment experienced by Presbyterian preachers, teachers, and missionaries as they settled into Mormon villages; the reports of rocks being thrown at their doors in the night, and windows breaking at their homes, churches, and schools. After repeating the exaggerated stories on both sides, Brackenridge dismisses such accounts, and instead champions those that illustrate the good people in each group, and those who reinforced the truth that, as they came to understand each other they got along very well. Brackenridge documents the changing accounts of the same stories over time, as both sides had to admit they had exaggerated some of them to win support from their various constituencies. He also clarifies that the threat of excommunication on the part of the Mormons was a haphazard tool used by some bishops, but certainly not all, to curb bad behavior of members. There is also evidence that some statements of excommunication were only hollow and unwarranted intimidations, as admitted by some bishops (Brakenridge 2011, 162–228).

In close proximity to Entry 2 discussed above, Oliverson specifically mentioned the name of the school teacher in Franklin: "Miss Nobles." She was, according to the Presbyterian Church's (1881) *Reports of the Board*, a young woman named Miss Anna Noble. The *Hand-book on Mormonism*[10] (1882, 81–82) describes her further: "The next group of stations consists of Franklin—where Miss Anna Noble teaches the school of 46 scholars and conducts a Sabbath school of 52 boys and girls" (*Hand-book* 1882, 81–82). Another resource, *Home Mission Monthly* (1887, 27), explained that a free school in Franklin, Idaho, was established because "a number of liberal families in Franklin…were very anxious for a school." It also explains that during the second year of that school's existence, "Miss Anna Noble took charge of the Franklin work, and accomplished a great deal of good in the years that she was stationed there" (*Home* 1887, 27). I also learned in earlier pages of this resource that "[conspicuous] among the teachers…was Miss Anna Noble, who for twenty-six years has given her life to mission work" (*Home* 1887, 29–30). Reading through these resources allows us to better understand the motivations of the Presbyterian Church in the United States, of its committed teachers, and of its enthusiastic evangelists in the Women's Board of Home Missions to secure teachers and Christian education for the children of that area. This has been very helpful to add context to events surrounding Entry 2 of Oliverson's *Diary* on January 17, 1881.[11]

Entry 2 was the result of some very strong desires of multiple groups: Group 1: Parents in Franklin, Idaho, where quality education for their children was inconsistent or nonexistent, wanted organized, consistent, good quality mission schools and well-trained teachers. As indicated above, some of these parents appealed to Reverend C. W. Parks in Logan, Utah, to establish a school in their community. Group 2: The Presbyterians, motivated by their wish to Christianize and Americanize the Mormons of Franklin, Idaho, established missions on the frontier. The best way they found to fulfill that wish was through education. As a consequence, they mobilized their collective funds and "teachers" and established schools for children, believing it was a means to separate them from their faith. Group 3: The Mormon Church wanted to protect its members, especially their children, from being unduly evangelized by Presbyterian teachers.

Better understanding of the historical events surrounding the Presbyterian schools established in Franklin, Idaho, gives context to the event recorded by Oliverson and his response to it. He chose to respond the way he did because he was part of Group 1. He wanted an education for his children. For him, the threat of excommunication was not a real one as he had been excommunicated three years earlier. On the other hand, the marginalization of his children and spouse for his failure to remove the children from the school was a possible reality. Also, the potential consequence of his children being Christianized and losing their faith in Mormonism because of their teachers was a real possibility. However, Oliverson's response indicated that the education of his children was more important than either of those potentially negative outcomes. With an education of some kind, his children would have the ability to choose appropriately for themselves. This was positive. Having decisions made for him by those who coercively threatened to cut him off with fear tactics was negative. As in his reaction to the *Mormon Tribune* issue, considered above in Entry 1, Oliverson testified to the individual's right to make his or her own choice or decision. He encouraged good behavior, but felt that the decision to choose and produce good behavior lay within the free individual who could think and act for him- or herself.

Oliverson's responses in both Entry 1 and Entry 2 demonstrate a characteristic that defined him throughout his life: a fierce sense of independence. Oliverson decided what he wanted to do and refused any other man or group the right to determine his course of action. Transcribing the diaries caused me to ask questions about what he recorded. My research helped me better understand Oliverson's *Diary* entries because I now could read them in the context of the events that were happening around him. Consequently, I now have a better sense of him as a person. In short, I consider him more than just a name on a page or a picture in a frame. I no longer consider him mean, nor am I scared by his picture. In fact, spending months in his *Diary*, transcribing each word, and taking yet more months to research and understand the events recorded, I have learned not to be afraid of James Oliverson. Along with these newly found pictures on the Internet, I have had the opportunity to view him differently.

Figure 2. James Oliverson

Figure 3. James and Caroline Oliverson

Figure 4. James and Caroline Oliverson

Figure 5. James Oliverson with his six sons

I connected with this man as I read of his lengthy vigils, sitting by the bedside of his sick son James night after night, trying to comfort the uncomfortable, while fervently pleading with the Lord to spare his oldest. I also learned that he possessed a spirit of gratitude as I read his acknowledgement of the Lord's hand in the eventual healing of his son. Transcribing the *Diary* gratefully led me to expand my perception of Oliverson. I learned that behind his hard, somewhat cold exterior beat the heart—the warm heart—of a caring and compassionate man.

I was especially touched to read his entries describing the years when his wife Caroline was bedridden. In these instances, like so many others, I was most impressed by the things I did not read. Oliverson did not wallow in self-pity. There are few things more difficult than coping with the emotional and physical stress of taking care of a bedridden wife for over two years. Yet Oliverson did this without complaining.

It is true that he expressed concern at being overburdened with taking care of too much, but he never criticized nor blamed his sick wife. This held true with all the setbacks and frustrations he experienced. He rarely talked about people behind their backs in his *Diary*. I found this quite remarkable. I am very certain that Oliverson had several run-ins with people, simply because he possessed such a strong, independent spirit. I am sure that on several occasions he became very upset with others, and it is probably equally true that they became very upset with him. However, he never blamed his frustration on anyone else. In several of his accounts, even in the cases when he enjoyed success, he was true to his sense of who he was and maintained his integrity. His sense of freedom, demonstrated by his strongly guarded independence, called for individuals to take responsibility for both the good and the bad. As I learned how he chose to overcome his challenges, how he dealt with the events he encountered in his life, I am better prepared to deal with the events that will occur in mine. For me, that is exactly the value of researching diaries. That is the value of discovering oneself.

NOTES

1. In addition to the two volumes of James Oliverson's diaries held by my grandmother (1884–1886 and 1886–1888), I found transcriptions or microfilmed copies of the following volumes of the diaries, which resulted in 12 volumes: 1852, 1870, 1873–1879, 1879–1880, 1880–1882, 1882–1884, 1888–1889, 1889–1891, 1891–1892, and 1892–1893. I found these at the Utah Historical Society, Utah State University's Merrill-Cazier Library, and in the photocopy collection of Ray Oliverson, a distant relative whom I met as a result of transcribing these diaries. In 1995, I finished transcribing and editing them and they were printed and bound in a single volume, *The Diaries of James Oliverson: A Quiet Voice in the Town of Franklin.* In 1997, a second edition of this work was revised and enlarged by my father, Allan C. Wright, including more footnotes to give historical context to many events described. Several of these second edition copies were given as gifts to local libraries and historical associations. The references made to Oliverson's diaries in this paper are pulled from this second edition and are simply identified in the paper by the date of diary entry.

2. The situation of the *Mormon Tribune,* and the dissent of its editors and publishers, William S. Godbe, Elias Lacy, Thomas Harrison, Edward W. Tullidge, and others, is indeed complex. As I have investigated further, I have learned more about these periodicals, the people behind them, and the New Movement which developed in the mid- to late-nineteenth-century Utah Territory. It represents a clash between Brigham Young's perception of the Mormon Zion and the perception of largely British converts to Mormonism who immigrated to the Utah Territory, became disenchanted with Young's perception, and challenged it. They became quite confrontational and were labeled as apostates. In his book, *Wayward Saints: The Godbeites and Brigham Young*, Ronald W. Walker (1998, xv) indicates that "The Godbeites opposed Young and his ideal community partly because they represented another strain of Mormonism, which I call 'British Mormonism.' Many of the New Movement men and women were products of the Saints' successful evangelizing of early Victorian Great Britain, and when these members traveled to Utah, they brought with them the values and practices of their earlier days. They prized the city life of their British nativity; they were drawn to ideas and the arts; and they relished public debate. They also remembered British Mormonism's simple biblical doctrines and its abundant display of spiritual gifts. Finally, these men and women were used to challenging the status quo in Great Britain. All these tendencies were hard to set aside once they arrived in Utah. Indeed, this British heritage helps to explain the Godbeites' reservations about Brigham Young's agrarian, practical kingdom, with its stress on conformity, obedience, and unity." This is the culture that James Oliverson came from as a British convert to Mormonism himself. He displayed some of the same characteristics as the members of the New Movement. Another great resource that sheds lights on this event is Walker's (1997) chapter, "William S. Godbe (1833–1902) and Elias Lacy Thomas Harrison (1830–1900)," found in *Dictionary of Heresy Trials in American Christianity*. This details the ecclesiastical trial of these two men which would determine their continued membership in the Church of Jesus Christ of Latter-day Saints. These two sources help give the researcher a good

understanding of the details underlying the basic positions of Young and the established Church, and how they contrast with those held by Godbe, Harrison, and others of the New Movement. In order to help the researcher also understand the periodicals created by the New Movement, and how they influenced the economic, political, social, and religious environments of the time, please see O. N. Malmquist (1971), *The First 100 Years: A History of The Salt Lake Tribune, 1871–1971*.

3. I was interested to learn what was said at this meeting, believing that Brigham Young certainly would chastise the Mormons in the area for subscribing to the *Mormon Tribune*. I found recorded in the *Deseret News*: "Monday, 20th June 1870. We drove over the mountain to Franklyn and held a meeting, the people being addressed by L. Snow, John Taylor, D.H. Wells, W. Woodruff, F.D. Richards, and President Young. President Young said the Saints should labor to obtain the Spirit of God, and, in all their labors, temporal and spiritual, they should follow the dictations of that Spirit. All persons are liable to be tempted, but there is no need to yield. If a man yield to evil and lose the spirit of God, after having received it, and turns traitor and denies his God and betrays his brethren, neither the Lord nor his people can ever have the same confidence in him again. Blessed is that man who keeps the commandments of God in all things. All have to be governed by law; all exalted beings have to abide a law, and so must we if we ever enjoy the glory possessed by them. The Lord is pleased with good order and refinement, and we should seek to imitate Him." (*Deseret News*, 298). This was a summary of Young's talk, and we don't have a summary of those given by the other speakers. I include it here because I was somewhat surprised that Brigham Young's counsel was not more hellfire and damnation. That was the portrait painted of Brigham Young by the dissenters, and I assumed he would live up to their caricature. However, I don't find evidence of that in this published summary of his remarks.

4. Levi was the son of Oliverson: Levi Roberts Oliverson (3 March, 1868–4 October, 1942).

5. Till and John are the children of James Oliverson: Matilda Oliverson (31 March, 1870–27 January, 1947) and John Besley Oliverson (22 February, 1872–26 October, 1941). They apparently received shoes from their schoolteacher Mrs. Martin, the wife of Mr. J. W. Martin, one of the Presbyterian teachers at Franklin and the brother of George Martin, the Presbyterian reverend located in Manti, Utah. The other teacher was Miss Anna Noble.

6. James was the son of James Oliverson: James Henry Oliverson (11 May, 1866–19 February, 1932). The teacher is Miss Anna Noble. A little bit more about the teaching career of Anna Noble can be found in "Teachers of Presbyterian Schools in Utah and Idaho" assembled by Fred Burton (2006). Miss Anna C. Noble came to Utah with teaching experience in Iowa. She began teaching in Springville, Utah, in 1877. She was assigned to Franklin, Idaho, in 1880 and taught there through 1886. She then moved to Wellsville, Utah, in 1886 and taught through 1893; moved to Samaria, Idaho, and taught from 1894 to 1899; and finally, moved to Kaysville, Utah, from 1899 to 1903, when she retired after twenty-six years of teaching in the Utah and Idaho Presbyterian schools. During retirement she collected relief grants. In 1908 she suffered from cataracts in both eyes and bronchial asthma. She died in 1914. Also teachers in the Franklin school were Miss Tillie (Lillie E.) Kelley (Kelly) from 1882 to 1884, a former student of Miss Noble's; Miss Ella M. (M. E.) Campbell from 1884 to 1885; Miss Jennie Simons (Simmons), an assistant teacher from 1885 to 1886; Miss Blenda (Balinda) Christine Johnson from 1898 to 1901; and Miss Harriet Elliott, another former student of Miss Noble's, from 1901 to 1905.

7. I found a teacher named Miriam Kelly in Burton's (2006) list but there was no mention of her working in Franklin.

8. Christopher and Will were sons of James Oliverson: Christopher Oliverson (29 December, 1876–12 September, 1934) and William Oliverson (2 August, 1879–9 June, 1932).

9. Richard was also a son of James Oliverson: Richard Thomas Oliverson (31 March, 1875–5 September, 1938).

10. Some attribute the *Hand-book* to J. M. Coyner, a Presbyterian leader in Utah, but it appears that he simply applied for the copyright with the Library of Congress.

11. To give the reader a feel for the sentiment of those involved in the Home Mission activities of the Presbyterian Church in the United States, we read the following from the *Reports of the Boards* (1881, 3–4): "It is not a new thing for this Board to call for more men for frontier work; but in view of such facts as have been named we desire to call the attention of the Assembly to the **growing demand for much more laborers**. The last year we obtained all the good men we could from the graduating classes in all our theological seminaries, but the supply was not equal to the demand, and we were constrained to send out, at heavy cost, many men with families, who on that account cannot as easily adapt themselves to frontier work. **But obtaining men from all available sources, we have been unable to acquire the requisite number.** This year the difficulty is not diminished. The railways are extending the people are still flocking into the newest portions of the west. The missionaries on the ground are constantly appealing for helpers and yet it is impossible to find the men we need. **Our financial condition seems to intimate what is The Divine will and the will of the Church on that subject.** The Treasurer's report shows that nearly $15,000 more has been raised the past year than any previous year in our history. **Is not such a result proof conclusive that the Lord and his people are urging us to press forward and occupy all the waste places of the Land? We therefore call on the Assembly to consider carefully the necessity for our increased supply of missionaries for the new States and territories—not as an exigency or a temporary but as a permanent necessity—for if this country is to be won for Christ, if we as a Church are to keep pace with the increase of population and its rapid flow in the vast and unoccupied spaces of our country, we must plan not for a single year but for decades—we must plan for an increasing demand for men till the population is equalized from sea to sea.** We desire to call the special attention of the assembly to the 'Present Outlook' of the work presented, being largely in the language of missionaries of experience who know whereof they affirm. It shows what wonderful opportunities are now furnished us for home missionary work." From the "Present Outlook" just referred to, we read: **"We desire to set before you as far as our space will allow in the language of missionaries of experience, who know whereof they affirm, the wonderful opportunities that are thus presented for home missionary work. Now is the time to make the desert blossom as the rose, to redeem wide wastes for the kingdom of the Redeemer.** By what is said below you will see that more men are called for in Dakota and Montana, Nebraska and Kansas, Texas and New Mexico, Colorado, Utah, California and Oregon. Shall such glorious opportunities be thrown away? Shall not the past suffice for the day of small things? **The people in the new sections, in the sparse settlements, in the wilderness, among the mountains, in the mining towns, need to be looked after** *now*. **Their children need Sabbath schools** *now*. **The church has money enough and men enough to fill the broad land with the institutions of the Gospel if she will only awake.** The writers show what has been accomplished in the past as an encouragement to undertake the larger work of the future" (5–6). From the section of the report entitled "Woman's Work. The Department of Schools" we read the following: "In the progress of our work, when our missionaries found themselves face to face with the Indians on their reservation, the Mormons of Utah, the Mexican in South Colorado, New Mexico and Arizona, **the necessity for Christian Schools as a means of evangelization became conspicuously apparent**. The matter was brought before the General Assembly, which virtually said: 'This work among the Mormons, the Mexicans and Indians is exceptional. The women, as a whole, have never taken any marked share in Home Missions, except in the preparation of 'Boxes' to add to the comfort of Home Missionary families. Let our women then assume the work; to them so strikingly appropriate, and support the mission schools called for. Let the Board of Home Missions go on to establish these schools so far as the women supply the means.' The Board of Home Missions accepted the trust. The Women already at work were inspirited to fresh effort. By recommendation of the General Assembly, twenty-seven of the Synods have appointed Synodical Committees of women to stimulate and superintend the work for Home Missions, of the women,

each within its limits. These Synodical Committees as a whole are organically conjoined in the Woman's Executive Committee of Home Missions, which was organized in answer to a general demand for woman's work exclusively for Home Missions.... Since the women of the Church began this work, it has gained in interest beyond all precedent. **The Government, the people at large, and especially the churches are turning their attention to Schools of the Indians, and churches are regarded as necessary to fit them for citizenship. So of the Mormons. All the people are growing indignant at the monstrous thing that sets itself up as the Church of God in Utah.** The railroads penetrating and crossing New Mexico open all its towns to new forms of business, and its valleys to the occupation of Northern men. **A new era is dawning. The people must fall into line, and keep step with the advancing civilization of the country. Schools are essential to their enlightenment and evangelization.** All this work everywhere may be greatly enlarged. A rising interest is felt in the church regarding it. **By the blessing of God this training of the young will make itself felt in the early future to the sapping of the foundations of superstition, ignorance and fake religion, and to the up-building of the cause and kingdom of our Redeemer.** These mission schools, although committed as above stated to hands so new to the work, have been manifestly owned of the Master, whose guidance and blessing in it should be acknowledged to the glory of His Holy Name. **They are nearly all so grouped that each school house is also a preaching station, and connected with them is also a Sabbath School.** The teachers in the government boarding schools are paid by the government, but we put in their names to show the entire civilizing and evangelizing force among all the tribes in which we are expending any labor" (26–27). In the appendix of this published report we read the following: "In Utah.—So among the Mormons in Utah, twice as large as Ohio. In the past few years the work of our Board in that benighted territory has immensely advanced. There exists one of the most prosperous, promising missions in our land. **Our schools unsettle the faith of the children in Mormonism—and many adults are found to confront the alienation of their property, as the price of the Christian confession.** There schools develop into churches as a rule. **They are an entering wedge to split parental opposition through children"** (119). I have used bold face in the quotes above to highlight the zeal with which the Home Mission of the Presbyterian Church was approaching this evangelization opportunity. Some of their comments, especially the stated intention of the Home Mission of the Presbyterian Church to unsettle the faith of the Mormon children and drive a wedge between children and their parents in their efforts to Americanize and Christianize the people, are very disturbing.

REFERENCES

Brackenridge, R. Douglas. 2011. "Hostile Mormons and Persecuted Presbyterians in Utah, 1870–1900: A Reappraisal." *Journal of Mormon History*, 37, no. 3: 162–228.

Brite, J. Duncan. 1956a. "Non-Mormon Schools and Churches." In *The History of a Valley: Cache Valley, Utah-Idaho*, edited by Joel E. Ricks, 303–20. Logan, Utah: Cache Valley Centennial Commission.

———. 1956b. "The Public Schools." In *The History of a Valley: Cache Valley, Utah-Idaho*, edited by Joel E. Ricks, 321–48. Logan, Utah: Cache Valley Centennial Commission.

Burton, Fred. 2006. "Teachers of Presbyterian Schools in Utah and Idaho." http://www.westminstercollege.edu/library/digitization/burton/Teachers List.pdf.

Corbetta, Piergiorgio. 2003. *Social Research: Theory, Methods and Techniques*. Translated by Bernard Patrick. London: SAGE Publications.

Davies, George K. 1945–1947. "A History of the Presbyterian Church in Utah." A reprint of a doctoral thesis appearing in the *Journal of the Presbyterian Historical Society* 23, no. 4: 228–48; 24, no. 3: 147–81; 24, No. 1: 44–68; 25, no. 1: 46–67. https://www.jstor.org/journal/jpreshistsoc.

The Deseret News. 1870. Weekly, vol. 19 (Monday, 20th June)

Hand-book on Mormonism. 1882. Salt Lake City: Handbook Publishing Company. https://books.google.com/books?id=_lY3AAAAMAAJ&pg=PP7#v=onepage &q&f=false.

Home Mission Monthly. 1887. 1, no. 12. https://books.google.com/books?id=oimYQV k2L4kC&pg=PA262#v=onepage&q&f=false.

Malmquist, O. N. 1971. *The First 100 Years: A History of The Salt Lake Tribune, 1871–1971.* Salt Lake City: Utah State Historical Society.

Oliverson, James. 1997. *The Diaries of James Oliverson: A Quiet Voice in the Town of Franklin.* Transcribed and edited by John B. Wright. 2nd ed. Revised and enlarged by Allan C. Wright. Provo, Utah: A. C. Wright.

Pimlott, B. 2002. "Dear Diary…." *The Guardian*, G2, 18 October.

Presbyterian Church in the U.S.A. (P.C.U.S.A.) 1881. *Reports of the Boards, volume 6.* New York: Presbyterian Church in the U.S.A. https://books.google.com /books?id=DWlJAAAAMAAJ&printsec=frontcover&source=gbs_ge_summary _r&cad=0#v=onepage&q&f=false.

Walker, Ronald W. 1998. *Wayward Saints: The Godbeites and Brigham Young.* Urbana and Chicago: University of Illinois Press.

———. 1997. "William S. Godbe (1833–1902) and Elias Lacy Thomas Harrison (1830–1900)." In *Dictionary of Heresy Trials in American Christianity*, edited by George H. Shriver, 150–59. Westport, Conn.: Greenwood Press.

5. Latino History Is Oregon History: Preserving Oregon's Latino Heritage through the Pineros y Campesinos Unidos del Noroeste Archive

David Woken
Sonia De La Cruz
Stephanie Kays

Introduction

Since the spring of 2011, the University of Oregon Libraries have been working closely with the Pineros y Campesinos Unidos del Noroeste (Northwest Tree Planters and Farmworkers United, PCUN) to organize, preserve, and make accessible to the public the extensive records they have generated during their history. A union of largely Latino farmworkers based in Oregon's fertile Willamette Valley, PCUN is the largest organization representing Oregon's growing Latino population. As in many other states, the state's Latino community is growing so rapidly that, as of the 2010 census, Latinos constitute Oregon's largest ethnic minority. Since 1985, PCUN has been a fierce advocate of the rights of farmworkers, 98 percent of whom are Latino. Engaged faculty at the University of Oregon have worked closely with PCUN over the years, advancing research and social justice through intellectual and activist collaboration. As PCUN has matured as an organization, it has increasingly recognized the need to preserve its own story, both for the institution's future and as a contribution to Oregon's Latino community. For its part, the University of Oregon (UO), as the flagship public university of the state of Oregon, has acknowledged the importance of recognizing and serving all segments of Oregon's diverse population. This convergence of interests led to the agreement between PCUN and the UO, signed in June of 2011, to house and make accessible to the public PCUN's records. Since that time, faculty, students, and staff at the UO Libraries have been working to organize and advocate for this important collection. Drawing on a network of engaged scholars, community

Who Are We Really?: Latin American Family, Local and Micro-Regional Histories, and Their Impact on Understanding Ourselves. Papers of the Fifty-Ninth Annual Meeting of SALALM, 2014.

activists, and skilled librarians, the PCUN records have been a nucleus for projects to ensure that UO truly serves all of the people of Oregon, and that the state's history does not marginalize its Latino community.

PCUN and Latino History in Oregon

PCUN was founded in 1985 as an extension of the work that the Willamette Valley Immigration Project (WVIP) had been doing since 1977, to support the largely immigrant farmworker population of Oregon's Willamette Valley. Migrant farmworkers, the vast majority of them Latino, had been the backbone of Oregon's farm labor force for decades. The WWII Bracero Program, active in the Pacific Northwestern states of Idaho, Oregon, and Washington from 1942 to 1947, helped to establish patterns of labor recruitment and migration that brought Latino laborers up the West Coast, as they followed the harvest looking for work (Gamboa 1990). Throughout the subsequent decades, migrant farmers from Mexico, Texas, California, and other western states "settled out" and began establishing a more permanent presence in Oregonian farming towns like Cornelius, Independence, and Woodburn, as well as larger cities like Portland, Salem, and Eugene.

The WVIP grew out of a series of initiatives throughout the 1960s and 1970s to improve the living and working conditions of farmworkers and, as part of the Chicano Movement, to pursue full civil rights and community self-determination for Oregon's growing Latino population (Gonzales-Berry and Mendoza 2010, 52–91). As that population grew and became more established, Latinos could be found in a growing range of professions and locations, from working-class occupations like farmworkers and pineros—tree planters contracted to restore clear-cut forests in the mountains of Oregon starting in the 1970s—to middle class professionals in education, law, business, and public service. WVIP activists gave free legal aid to Latinos facing deportation and labor exploitation, especially farmworkers and pineros. As the 1980s rolled on, however, they recognized the need to provide services beyond legal aid. So, PCUN drew specific inspiration from the example of the United Farmworkers movement in California, and was incorporated as a farmworkers' labor union at a founding convention, in Woodburn, Oregon, on September 15, 1985 (Stephen 2012, 16).

In the thirty years since then, PCUN has grown to be the largest group to represent Oregon's Latino community. In addition to its work organizing in the forests and fields of the Willamette Valley, among many other organizations, PCUN helped found Causa, Oregon's largest immigrants' rights organization; the Farmworker Housing Development Corporation, a high-quality affordable housing project for farmworkers based in Woodburn; and KPCN-LP, Radio Movimiento, one of the nation's first low-power FM radio stations. In addition, PCUN has played a major role in Oregon politics, helping influence fights over bilingual education, labor rights and a minimum wage, and immigrants' rights in the state. It has been a major ally of environmental organizations seeking to regulate pesticides, and has long allied with Basic Rights Oregon, the state's largest LGBT-advocacy organization, to fight homophobia and defend immigrants' rights in the state (Stephen 2012). Having played such an important role in so many aspects of the state's social, political, and cultural life over such a long period, PCUN's records, which include materials dating back to the 1960s, are crucial to provide a picture of Oregon's history, one that includes all of its people.

Appraisal, Acquisition, and Processing of the PCUN Records

> Archivists appraise, collect, and preserve the props with which notions of identity are built. In turn, notions of identity are confirmed and justified as historical documents validate their authority. (Kaplan 2000)

In December of 2010, James Fox, Linda Long, Cassie Schmitt, and Kira Homo, of the UO Special Collections & University Archives (SCUA) curatorial and technical team, traveled to Woodburn, Oregon. They met with PCUN's then secretary-treasurer Larry Kleinman for a tour of PCUN's archival facilities and storage areas. The main objective of the visit was to conduct a field appraisal of PCUN's physical and electronic records. Within an archival context, appraisal is a process of identifying what records exist or are being offered and determining whether those records and other documentary materials have enduring, historical value. There are a number of factors to take into consideration while making appraisal decisions, which may include functional characteristics, or who created the record and why; which actions are being documented; analysis of records in the context of other related documentary resources; potential uses of the records; limitations on access to those records, e.g., legal, medium, privacy issues; and the cost of preservation weighed against the information value of the record (Ham 1993).

One of the fundamental methods archivists use in the selection process is the records survey, in which they gather basic information about an organization and its records. With records kept in various storage rooms, offices, and closets, the SCUA staff conducted a survey to gather information about PCUN's records, including quantity, form, document types, physical condition, location, the way in which materials were stored, and the creator and/or function related to the records. Overall, they surveyed approximately 240 linear feet of records. These included paper files, audiotapes, videotapes, DVDs, photographs and negatives, digital records, posters, ephemera, and a few artifacts. The survey not only facilitated a better understanding of the scope and contents of PCUN's records, but also provided pertinent information to help SCUA plan for eventualities, including physical space to store the material, potential preservation and access, and the funding needed to sustain all of the above long-term.

Benefits of the UO-PCUN Relationship

Unions that generate and maintain their records eventually face the choice to support their own in-house archives program or to develop a relationship with an established collecting repository (Nash 2010, 15). The latter is a common avenue among unions and it has some clear benefits. In the case of the PCUN-UO partnership, one of the benefits for PCUN is the maintenance of their organization's history and its materials. Also, as the UO Libraries provide the infrastructure to appropriately preserve and provide access to the records over time, PCUN is in the distinct position of preserving and sharing their records with the public. These benefits include secure, climate-controlled storage; curators of various media and digital records, some of which are approaching obsolescence; and a professional reference staff who can connect diverse communities to the records through finding aids, researcher services, and other outreach efforts.

On the other hand, some of the concerns from the union's perspective may be the general accessibility of their historical records to union membership, officers, and staff, and the specific loss of control over that access. Given the legal character and privacy concerns associated with certain records generated by PCUN over the years, such as notes from collective bargaining sessions, strategic organizing meetings, or other issues related to citizenship and members' immigration status, PCUN must retain the confidentiality of those documents for some time. We addressed these concerns as we developed the PCUN-UO partnership, through a strong access policy and a shared desire to bring PCUN's story and contributions to the labor movement and the public.

The acquisition of the PCUN records is equally an asset for the UO Libraries' Special Collections & University Archives department. The long-term partnership that the UO faculty has developed with PCUN is in clear alignment with the UO Libraries' Strategic Directions (UOL 2012) in a number of ways. The PCUN archive enhances our contribution to scholarship and a dynamic teaching environment, and fosters access to primary sources and encourages their use in classroom instruction. Also, with the growth of Oregon's Latino population, the University of Oregon anticipates a rise in the population of Latino students at the university and is striving to increase Latino representation on campus. The records in this collection bring to light the work and activities of PCUN and the history of Latinos in Oregon more broadly. It is important for the UO Libraries to continue developing its Latino collections, making them more visible to students and the community. The PCUN records also contribute to the diversity of SCUA's collections and contribute to a more inclusive campus environment.

PCUN Records and the OLHC Graduate Teaching Fellow

In 2011, PCUN and SCUA selected and transferred approximately twenty linear feet of materials to the UO Libraries, with additional accretions scheduled for the coming years. While this represents only a fraction of the records initially surveyed in 2010, they document some of the union's key initiatives. In celebration of the PCUN-UO partnership and the transfer of records, the UO Libraries' Manuscript Curator, Linda Long, designed a digital exhibit (https://blogs.uoregon.edu/pcun/) of the PCUN records. It detailed the evolution of PCUN, farmworker living and working conditions, the activities of the WVIP, and many of the union's political and workplace organizing campaigns. However, at the start of 2013, with the celebrations and transfer of a year's worth of records, there was still only a basic, unpublished inventory and the records were still virtually unknown to most students and scholars at the university. In the fall of 2013, the Oregon Latino Heritage Collaborative (OLHC) received support from the University of Oregon to help fund a graduate teaching fellow (GTF) for nine months. Led by the UO Libraries, the fellow would help assess the PCUN records and other manuscript collections containing Latino materials; create a finding aid for the PCUN records to be published on the Northwest Digital Archives (NWDA) website; improve existing finding aids to other Latino collections in SCUA; work with library and OLHC staff to update web pages promoting the collections; and, through outreach efforts, enhance the use of the materials in UO classrooms and within the community.

Sonia De La Cruz began working at SCUA as the OLHC's GTF in September of 2013. Then a doctoral candidate at the School of Journalism and Communication, her research combined theoretical and practical approaches to understanding how the Latino diaspora shapes identity and builds community through media. Additionally, De La Cruz has been involved in documenting and preserving Latino history in Oregon for a number of years. She was the clear choice to fulfill this GTF role because of her past work and knowledge of union operations, her ability to work with multilingual collections, and her connection to the OLHC and many of its stakeholders. The unprocessed PCUN records provided the original impetus for the OLHC fellowship, and De La Cruz spent much of her time working with this collection. She created a bilingual finding aid for the PCUN records and worked with David Woken, SCUA's then-director James Fox, and others in the OLHC, to reach out to university faculty and students and Oregon's Latino community.

The Jefferson Center for Education and Research Records and the John Little Papers were two other collections in SCUA's repository that were further advanced through De La Cruz's work with the OLHC fellowship. The Jefferson Center for Education and Research, which operated from 1994 to 2007, "specialized in facilitating discussion, problem solving and community connections among low-income non-timber forest workers and harvesters, rural communities and contingent laborers in the Pacific Northwest" (UOL-SCUA 2014a). The center's records were donated in two batches, the first in 2004 by the organization's founder, Beverly A. Brown, and the second in 2009 on behalf of the center, by Sarah Loose. Much of this collection was processed and made accessible to the public in 2011, with the exception of 4.5 linear feet of records that included administrative files of the Jefferson Center, and its correspondence with Latino groups in Oregon. These records were processed and added to the collection in the spring of 2014.

John Little donated his papers to the university in 2010, and they were processed and made accessible in 2011. He was the executive director of the Valley Migrant League (VML) and one of the founding members of the Colegio César Chávez in Mount Angel, Oregon. The VML was a private, non-profit organization that ran from 1965 to 1974. It "helped Oregon migrant farm workers and former farm workers attain a better life through education and social services," and was instrumental in establishing a strong Latino community in the Willamette Valley (UOL-SCUA 2014b). Named for the Mexican American civil rights activist and union organizer, the Colegio César Chávez was established in 1973 and closed in 1983. It was the first accredited, independent, four-year Chicano/Latino higher education institution in the United States (Maldonado 2000; May 2011, 135–259). During her appointment to the OLHC fellowship, De La Cruz worked with the John Little Papers to add further information to their finding aid, and provide context to Little's role in both of these organizations.

Elevating Oregon's Latino History through Archives

Along with their community partners, UO faculty from several academic units have made significant strides toward fostering Latino heritage projects and expanding Latino and Latin American scholarship. Their numerous Latino-related projects include research, courses, exhibits, and events, including the "Latino Roots" course and the acquisition of the PCUN records. These projects have been crucial toward elevating Latino history in Oregon and have enabled UO to build ties with the Latino community across the state.

On June 6, 2011, UO celebrated the "PCUN-UO Partnership" in a public event at the Knight Library. Then UO President Richard Lariviere and PCUN President Ramón Ramírez signed a deed of gift, in which PCUN donated its historic records to SCUA to be processed, preserved, and made available to the public. The event also showcased the documentary films UO students produced in the university's "Latino Roots," a two-quarter course taught by Professors Lynn Stephen, from the Department of Anthropology, and Gabriela Martínez, from the School of Journalism and Communication. This course was designed to broaden Oregon's historical narrative by documenting the depth and breadth of Latino and Latin American immigration, settlement, and social movements, as well as to highlight Latinos' civic and political actions and contributions to the state (Martínez and Stephen 2015). To document and expand Oregon's dominant historical narrative, largely centered on the Anglo-American pioneer experience, students learn about the larger racial, ethnic, and colonial narratives of the state by carrying out research and conducting oral history interviews.

In addition, students produce short digital documentary films to narrate the stories of contemporary Latino immigrants across Oregonian generations and geography. At the end of the course, students screen their documentaries at a public event.

In 2011, as part of the PCUN-UO Partnership celebration, students from the "Latino Roots" course showcased sixteen short documentary films. Among the many attendees were students, deans, administrators, faculty, Latino leaders, community members, farmworker families, elected officials, and the people and families whose stories were narrated in the films. In addition to the screenings, students donated their films to the UO Libraries as a symbolic gesture in support of their work to enhance Latino history and research at the university. Today, these films are part of the university's archives and are available for public use (Martínez and Stephen 2015). This event cemented a bond between the university and Oregon's Latino community. For this reason two subsequent classes of "Latino Roots" students held public screenings on June 6, 2013 and June 4, 2015, respectively, to showcase an additional nineteen and seventeen films about Latino history in Oregon. So far, students have produced fifty-two short documentary films and many more will be produced as the course is taught in coming years.[1]

The success of the "Latino Roots" 2011 public event, coupled with increased public interest in projects which documented histories and stories of Oregon's Latino population, prompted faculty and community leaders to develop a working group to continue expanding Latino-related projects at the UO. In November of 2011, university and community partners established the Oregon Latino Heritage Collaborative (OLHC), to support the expansion of Latino heritage projects in which the community and the academy could join in conversation and collaborate. The OLHC would coordinate UO Latino heritage projects until the fall of 2014.

The mission of the OLHC supported "opening new avenues to preserve, share, research, study and narrate Latino communities' history as Oregon and American history" (OLHC 2014). The OLHC shared a vision of engaging across disciplines with current and future university students, researchers, educators, and writers, along with political and civic leaders and community members who can contribute to knowledge about Oregon Latino history, and therefore help strengthen bonds between themselves and the university. The OLHC's founding members included James Fox, then head of SCUA; Gabriela Martínez, associate professor in the School of Journalism and Communication at UO; Larry Kleinman, president of CAPACES Leadership Institute (an organization affiliated with PCUN), and then secretary-treasurer of PCUN; Antonio Huerta, opportunities outreach manager, Division of Undergraduate Studies at UO; and Elias Meyer, assistant director for the Center for Latino/a and Latin American Studies (CLLAS) at UO (see Chart 1). The steering committee consisted of university and community partners who represented the following organizations and academic units: Oregon Folklife Network, UO Labor Education and Research Center, UO Latin American Studies Program, Amigos Multicultural Services Center, UO Libraries, CAPACES Leadership Institute, PCUN, and CLLAS.

Chart 1. Core members comprising the OLHC

The OLHC took flight when it acquired the PCUN records and continued to support the processing and promotion of the archive, as well as to engage in other Latino heritage projects across the campus. With the assistance of its GTF, De La Cruz, the PCUN records were processed and catalogued during the winter and spring of 2013–2014. Since then there has been a great deal of outreach to make the collection more visible and accessible to the community, UO faculty, and the PCUN leadership, and to discuss the contents and arrangement of the records and how they can be used both in UO classes and by the general public. To generate greater awareness of the collection among university and community partners, an open house event was organized in which students, local community leaders, and members of the PCUN were invited to see the primary documents and learn more about the collection. The open house took place on May 7, 2014 in SCUA's Paulson Reading Room, where a number of documents from the PCUN collection were put on display and the bilingual finding aid was announced to the public. Additionally, out of the success of the "Latino Roots" documentary projects, the OLHC advised and collaborated with UO's Oregon Folklife Network to develop "Telling our Stories"

(OFN 2015), an online toolkit designed to teach people of varied skills and ages how to document personal, community, or family stories.

The PCUN-UO partnership was significant because it marked the beginning of a relationship between the university and the Latino community, but also because it sparked ongoing contributions to the university's dual mission of academic excellence and diversity. The aid of supporting entities like the OLHC, faculty, students, and community partners, contributed to the expansion of archival records documenting the Latino experience in Oregon. Having helped establish a strong set of projects to forward our understanding of Oregon's Latino heritage at the UO, the OLHC disbanded in the fall of 2014 and its activities were largely taken up by CLLAS through its Latino History Research Action Project. Since then, UO scholars, librarians, archivists, and community leaders have continued to identify related collections at other institutions and obtain new ones. These will ensure that the stories of Oregon's Latino community become an integral part of Oregon's history.

The PCUN Records Reach Faculty, Students, and the Community

One of the important factors in PCUN's decision to house its archive at the University of Oregon was that, as a public institution, UO would make the archive accessible to a broad public. However, the fact that so much of the collection consisted of copyrighted materials like newspaper or magazine clippings, made and continues to make its mass digitization a difficult proposition. Faced with this limitation, UO librarians and archivists have pursued a broad, systematic outreach program to bring the archive into use by UO faculty, students, and the broader community. Relying on a strong foundation of faculty support for the archive and their interest in using its documents in their classes, the OLHC set out in the winter and spring sessions of 2014 to identify the faculty who gave courses and assignments in which particular sections of the collection could be especially useful. Through these outreach efforts, the OLHC recruited faculty to use the collection as early as spring of 2014, and others followed suit in the 2014–2015 academic year.

In seeking how to make the PCUN records more accessible to the public, the OLHC wanted to move beyond traditional research uses in graduate or upper level undergraduate courses in history, Latino studies, or labor studies courses. These subjects would be important constituencies for the collection, of course, but considering that the collection's materials related to politics, environmental activism, communications, and many other fields, the OLHC wanted to be sure that creative scholars could incorporate those materials into their courses, as well. Growing pedagogical trends in the humanities and social sciences cultivate information literacy and critical thinking through hands-on work with primary source materials. Considering those trends, the OLHC focused its outreach so that scholars in diverse fields could use primary source materials found in the PCUN records in their classes. They were also interested in how undergraduate or even secondary students might use the materials.

To this end, De La Cruz and Woken met with faculty in various fields to find matches between their course work and the materials held in the PCUN records. Initially, this meant meeting with faculty who were already using special collections in their courses, outside the usual advanced research seminar model. De La Cruz communicated with a faculty member in English literature about how she had used primary documents in her feminist science fiction course. The students completed an assignment in which they consulted the Ursula K. Le Guin Papers housed in SCUA, used them to edit Wikipedia entries on related subjects and write reports, and then posted them on a shared course blog, the *Feminist Science Fiction Seminar* (https://femscifi.wordpress.com/). These short assignments provided a model that worked well within lower level undergraduate courses. This helped us conceptualize the scale of this kind of assignment when we developed examples for faculty interested in using the collections for short research assignments with undergraduate students.

Woken met with Marsha Weisiger, an historian who specializes in the environment and the American West, and uses special collection materials in two of her undergraduate courses. Regarding US environmental history, Weisiger worked with SCUA to identify several collections of papers from lumber companies or entrepreneurs that were now held in the University of Oregon's collections. She had students use those papers to write short micro-histories of elements of local environmental history and how they fit within the broader range of themes identified in the class. In her course on the history of the American West she had students select an Oregon Trail diary from SCUA's collections and write a paper that analyzed it within the context of the history they had studied. In all of these cases, we saw that faculty were using archives to give students rich experiences with primary source materials, applying the critical skills of original historical or literary research in small assignments. This fostered not only knowledge of the subject matter, but skills which would serve them in future work at the UO.

With these lessons in mind, we then combed through the emerging finding aid of the PCUN records to identify themes, both in terms of subject matter—immigration, legislative battles, environmental issues—and of usefulness to particular disciplines—communications, political science, and others—around which we might present the archive to faculty. We selected six faculty in Journalism and Communication, Environmental Studies, Education, Literature, and Labor Studies to reach out to and discuss the ways in which they or their departmental colleagues might use the archive in their undergraduate courses. Throughout our meetings with faculty we gained useful insights into the type of opportunities the PCUN records provided for undergraduate students. We were not surprised to find there was much excitement among scholars interested in historical subjects, social movements, and even environmental studies, to use the archive in their courses. However, we did find less interest than we had hoped for when we spoke with professors in communications and education, areas in which our ideas were a bit less traditional. We also did not hear back from two faculty with whom we had hoped to meet. Still, we now had some idea of what parts of the collection were interesting to faculty, and some compelling ways they could use the archive in undergraduate and other lower level courses.

An opportunity to use the collection in an undergraduate course fell into our laps with a first-year faculty member in the History Department. As the first ever Latino history hire in that department,[2] this historian taught a freshman Latino history course in the spring 2014 session. Woken met with her in March of 2014, a month before UO's spring session began, and worked with her to design an assignment using the PCUN archive. Since the collection covers material from roughly the 1960s to the present, with its vast majority from the 1980s, 1990s, and 2000s, the assignment would need to come near the end of the course and be short enough to complete in two or three weeks. In the end, the students worked in groups to select a single document from the PCUN records, used the archive's finding aid and UO anthropologist Lynn Stephen's (2012) short history of PCUN, and created short group presentations they would give in class. The students had an instruction session showing them how to use the archive and its finding aid. They also had the chance to analyze some sample pieces pulled from the archive on May 7, the day of the PCUN records' open house and the first one that the archive was officially open for consultation. Though the class was composed entirely of freshmen and sophomores who had never used archives before, they successfully navigated the records to find primary sources that deepened their understanding of the subject matter and how it was expressed in a local context. This class opened doors to several other courses as this professor returned to work with the PCUN records in a course she co-taught in winter 2015. Her colleague was a UO sociolinguist who studied Spanish and Spanglish among US immigrant populations, who also ended up using the collection in a spring 2015 course she taught about Spanglish. Active outreach had brought in faculty from linguistics to use a historical archive, a process we had rarely encountered before at the UO Libraries.

In addition to these classes, we were able to inspire interest in the archive for several other UO courses in the 2014–2015 year. The undergraduate "Immigrants and the Farmworker Movement" and "Latino Roots" courses, taught by Lynn Stephen and Stephen and Gabriela Martínez, respectively, made heavy use of the archive. Other courses are now expressing interest, including some at institutions other than UO, and we have been actively working toward making the records available to nonacademic institutions, though those efforts are still in their very early stages. All of these courses will ensure that students use the archive, but will also provide us with further examples and models that we can apply in projects beyond traditional academic instruction and research.

The PCUN records outreach strategy also involved direct targeting of undergraduate and graduate students. De La Cruz and Woken met with students from the UO chapter of the Movimiento Estudiantil Chicano de Aztlán (MEChA). As in many other universities, the growth and sustained presence of Latino studies has been in part the work of engaged students, a relationship the OLHC recognized and that UO's Latino studies faculty hopes to continue to encourage. The PCUN records open house had a significant MEChA presence, and some students informally expressed interest in using the PCUN records for undergraduate thesis projects. In addition, since the open house event, David Woken has been approached by undergraduate and graduate students who want to use the archive for thesis work. It is clear now that this strategy of broad outreach through discussions with faculty, meetings with student organizations, and hosting public events, has created a wide-ranging knowledge of and interest in the PCUN records, at least on the UO campus.

The OLHC's outreach campaign also enjoyed a measure of success with groups beyond campus. Oportunidades is the Latino outreach arm of the University of Oregon's Opportunities Program, which aims to bring students from underrepresented Oregon communities to the UO (UO 2015). They have used interviews and oral histories gathered in the "Latino Roots" courses to supplement their materials, and have expressed interest in adding materials from the PCUN records to the traveling exhibits they present around the state. There have also been talks with members of the CAPACES Leadership Institute, to find ways to incorporate PCUN records materials into their courses. CAPACES is a youth education and training organization started by PCUN for young activists and the children of farmworkers (CLI 2015). The PCUN records have also been a beacon for others looking to preserve their personal collections of primary source materials about Oregon's Latino heritage. Several potential donors have approached Woken about collections of materials on Oregon's Latino community that they would like to deposit in SCUA's collections. The PCUN records are in the UO Libraries' hands to preserve and make them available for the community to use, so this kind of giving back is essential to assuring that these kinds of fruitful collaborations continue.

This work with faculty and students on the UO's campus, and with community education and outreach programs, is also helping to shape the possible directions that UO librarians, archivists, and faculty will take the archive in the future. Previously, CLLAS has organized training institutes for Oregon secondary school faculty at UO, and taught the history, culture, and social life of Oregon's growing Latino minority. CLLAS has been talking about doing so again sometime in the coming years. The PCUN records would be an important new addition to this training, providing teachers with the hands-on experience of working with primary source materials about Latino Oregon. Continued networking with community members beyond campus, including with librarian colleagues at other universities, community colleges, and public libraries in the region, will also help continued outreach regarding the collection, and help change the way people think about Oregon, its people, and their history.

Conclusion

In sum, outreach efforts with the PCUN records have taught UO librarians, archivists, and faculty that leveraging local interest, expertise, and vision is crucial. The time spent identifying faculty and students who are interested in the collection has paid off in assuring that the PCUN records are used. In particular, faculty who may not have otherwise thought to use the archive have expressed interest in doing so, as have those who seek to use it with lower-level students who might not normally be the expected audience for this kind of collection. Leveraging library subject specialists, existing networks with student organizations, and engaged faculty and graduate students, produced some deep interest in the collection. It also looks to be the main means through which interest in collections about Oregon's Latino heritage will continue to grow. Advertising and "marketing" the collection is important, but it is through thoughtful, direct engagement in social networks of scholars, activists, and involved community members, that we have generated the most interest in using and expanding the UO Libraries' Latino history collections.

Oregon is increasingly diverse, and its diverse people's histories need to be fully represented and understood. The PCUN records are at the vanguard of the UO Libraries' push to identify, gather, and offer materials about Oregon's Latino history. PCUN chose to house their archive at the UO in the hopes that it would be widely accessible. That way could help Oregon's Latino community, so long at the margins of mainstream consciousness, to enjoy a place in the story of Oregon. In order to ensure that happens, it is now incumbent upon us to help document the growth and dynamism of Latino Oregon.

NOTES

1. The "Latino Roots" course at the University of Oregon was first taught in 2011, then again in 2013 and 2015, and will continue to be taught every other subsequent academic year.

2. Previous Latino history specialists had been hired in other departments like Ethnic Studies.

REFERENCES

CLI (CAPACES Leadership Institute). 2015. "CAPACES Leadership Institute." http://www.capacesleadership.org/.

Gamboa, Erasmo. 1990. *Mexican Labor and World War II: Braceros in the Pacific Northwest, 1942–1947.* Austin: University of Texas Press.

Gonzales-Berry, Erlinda, and Marcela Mendoza. 2010. *Mexicanos in Oregon: Their Stories, Their Lives.* Corvallis: Oregon State University Press.

Ham, F. Gerald. 1993. *Selecting and Appraising Archives and Manuscripts.* Chicago: Society of American Archivists.

Kaplan, Elisabeth. 2000. "We Are What We Collect, We Collect What We Are: Archives and the Construction of Identity." *The American Archivist* 63:126–51.

Maldonado, Carlos S. 2000. *Colegio Cesar Chavez, 1973–1983: A Chicano Struggle for Educational Self-Determination.* New York: Garland Publishing.

Martínez, Gabriela and Lynn Stephen. 2015. "Our Course." Accessed July 14, 2015. http://latinoroots.uoregon.edu/our-course/.

May, Glenn Anthony. 2011. *Sonny Montes and Mexican American Activism in Oregon.* Corvallis: Oregon State University Press.

Nash, Michael. 2010. "Labor History and Archival Management." In *How to Keep Union Records*, edited by Michael Nash, 77–88. Chicago: Society of American Archivists.

OFN (Oregon Folklife Network). 2015. "Telling Our Stories Toolkit." Accessed July 14, 2015. https://blogs.uoregon.edu/toolkit/.

OLHC (Oregon Latino Heritage Collaborative). 2014. "Mission." Accessed August 13, 2014. http://olhc.uoregon.edu/mission-2/ (site discontinued).

Stephen, Lynn. 2012. *The Story of PCUN and the Farmworker Movement in Oregon.* Rev. ed. Eugene: Dept. of Anthropology, University of Oregon. http://cllas.uoregon.edu/wp-content/uploads/2010/06/PCUN_story_WEB.pdf.

UO (University of Oregon). 2015. "Opportunities." Accessed July 14, 2015. http://opportunities.uoregon.edu/.

UOL (University of Oregon Libraries). 2012. "UO Libraries Strategic Directions." Last modified August 21, 2012. https://library.uoregon.edu/general/about/mission.html.

UOL-SCUA (University of Oregon Libraries, Special Collections & University Archives). 2014a. "Guide to the Jefferson Center for Education and Research Records, 1935–2009." Accessed July 14, 2015. http://archiveswest.orbiscascade.org/ark:/80444/xv84390.

———. 2014b. "Guide to the John Little Papers, 1965–2006." Accessed July 14, 2015. http://archiveswest.orbiscascade.org/ark:/80444/xv64572.

6. An Intellectual History of Dominican Migration to the United States

Nelson Santana

Introduction

People who trace their ancestry to the Dominican Republic comprise the largest Latino immigrant group in New York City, with 604,844 residing among its five boroughs. A total of 1,208,060 more Dominicans live throughout the United States (Hernández and Stevens-Acevedo 2011, 484–85). In the twentieth and twenty-first centuries people of Dominican ancestry have more visibly penetrated mainstream US culture. As Hollywood's "Queen of Technicolor," the *barahonera*,[1] María Montéz's "exotic beauty" captivated silver screen viewers while television emerged and its popularity rose.

Porfirio Rubirosa was recognized as a jet-setting diplomat and prototypical playboy, whose sexual exploits were unrivaled in the twentieth century. His male genitalia alone were more newsworthy than other aspects of prominent figures among his generation. According to some sources, Ian Fleming's "James Bond" was in part inspired by Rubirosa.

Affectionately labeled the "Dominican Dandy," Hall of Fame pitcher Juan Marichal wooed baseball purists during the sixties and seventies by winning more games than any other pitcher during that time span (Lowe 1998).

In more recent times, Pulitzer-Prize winner Junot Díaz, author of the novel *The Brief Wondrous Life of Oscar Wao* (2007), became only the second person of Latino origin to be awarded that prize.

Lastly there was Aventura, a *bachata* group of reinvented Americans. They transformed a traditional musical genre once ostracized by Dominican society into a global phenomenon, and thus emerged internationally as the twenty-first century's undisputed kings of Dominican music. Not only have people of Dominican ancestry influenced mainstream US arts and sports markets, they have also interjected themselves into its politics. Many are aware that, in 1991, Guillermo Linares was the first person of Dominican ancestry to be elected into public office in New York City government, and soon after scores of Dominicans followed.[2] Notwithstanding these recent achievements, it was the organizing of Dominicans in the later twentieth and early

Who Are We Really?: Latin American Family, Local and Micro-Regional Histories, and Their Impact on Understanding Ourselves. Papers of the Fifty-Ninth Annual Meeting of SALALM, 2014.

twenty-first centuries—through the Centro Cívico Cultural Dominicano and the Club Cívico y Cultural Juan Pablo Duarte, for example—that facilitated the election of Dominicans into public office. Nearly all of the aforementioned Dominicans migrated to the United States after the 1950s. Two questions must be asked: from where did these people come, and why did so many people migrate from the Dominican Republic?

Quisqueya/Ayití

The Caribbean is home to the island originally baptized as Quisqueya and Ayití, by the Taínos who populated the Island prior to the arrival of the Europeans. Similar to other regions in Latin America, most historical and anecdotal accounts within the Island came from Europeans—mostly Spaniards—such as Bartolomé de las Casas. As the story goes, in 1492, Christopher Columbus arrived on the Island. Upon their arrival, the Spaniards mostly encountered the Taínos. This indigenous population were not as docile as sometimes portrayed by scholars. For instance, the *cacique* or chief, Guarocuya—also known as Enriquillo, the Spanish name by which he was baptized—fought the Spanish forces in Quisqueya. Both caciques in their own right, his aunt, Anacaona and her husband, Caonabo also fought the invaders.

The Taíno population started to rapidly decline due to their vulnerability to the Spaniards' foreign diseases, coupled with the harsh slave labor they were forced to endure. When the conquistadors recognized the decline, a new group of people was kidnapped and relocated to continue the inhumane labor. Spanish friar Bartolomé de las Casas is often believed to have convinced the Roman Catholic Church to spare the Taínos from that labor by recommending that African slaves be imported to the Americas. The massive incorporation of people from Western and Central Africa into the Western Hemisphere began the eventual genetics of Dominican society, whose people were and continue to be the product of three main cultures: Arawak, European—mostly Spanish—and African.

Today the Island is divided into two nations: the eastern side is known as Haiti while the western, comprising roughly two-thirds, is the Dominican Republic. What today is referred to as "Dominican identity" was constructed during the early and mid-nineteenth century. Haiti became a sovereign nation between 1803 and 1804, when it defeated France's mighty forces in the event that rocked the world: the Haitian Revolution (1791–1804). That created a domino effect that resonated throughout Latin America, as other nations followed suit by fighting for and successfully winning their independence. However, in order to prevent France, Spain, or any other European nation from recolonizing the Island, Haitian forces occupied the Spanish-speaking side, Santo Domingo, from 1822 through 1844.

A sense of Dominican empowerment and identity emerged during this period when, led by Juan Pablo Duarte and other Dominicans, Santo Domingo fought and gained its independence from Haiti on February 27, 1844. Not long after, Spanish Pedro Santana killed or exiled the leaders of the movement and annexed Santo Domingo to Spain. However, between 1863 and 1865, Dominicans fought for their second independence by defeating Pedro Santana and the Spanish forces. General Gregorio Luperón spearheaded and won that war, and subsequently became the first black president of the Dominican Republic in 1879.

The Earliest Dominicans

The city of Santo Domingo is considered by many to be the original city of the Americas, while New York City is often referred to as the capital of the world. In part, this can be attributed to the rich culture established through the comingling of different ethnic groups, thus making the City the migration epicenter. Washington Heights is to Dominicans as Harlem is to African Americans. In fact, the notion of Dominicans as "new immigrants" in the twentieth century is as intangible as Zeus' thunderbolt or the myth of the *ciguapa* housewife.[3]

Dominicans are often referred to or depicted in the media as "new Americans," as evident in publications such as *Multicultural America: An Encyclopedia of the Newest Americans* (2011). While that source and other scholars in the United States tend to refer to Dominicans as relatively new, this logic is incorrect. People born on the Island were American long before any immigrant or their children born in the United States were considered so. Doesn't the concept of the Americas begin in the Caribbean? According to Edmundo O'Gorman (1958), "America" was an invention as opposed to a discovery.

The presence of people from Hispaniola or Quisqueya in New York City can be traced back to 1613, when the first known person from Santo Domingo set foot on United States soil, thus preceding the official founding of the City.

In 1624, eighteen families accompanied Dutch Captain Cornelis Jacobsen May to settle in a region along the west bank of a river which eventually became known as the Hudson, and in 1626, the Dutch purchased the territory that would become New York (Burrows and Wallace 1999, 20, 23–26). At the time, the region was populated by the Lenape people (Stevens-Acevedo, Álvarez Francés, and Weterings 2013, 2).

Sailors of African ancestry—free men—traveled to the Americas alongside the earliest European explorers in 1492 (Moore and Clark 2012, 28). A free black man born in Santo Domingo traveled to the yet-unnamed territory 111 years later. By the time New York was founded, the first migrant from Santo Domingo had already set foot on the territory.

As Anthony Stevens-Acevedo (2013, 2) notes, the umbilical cord that connects people of Dominican ancestry to New York was formed upon the arrival of Juan Rodríguez—sometimes spelled Yan (for the Dutch "Jan")

Rodrigues—the first official immigrant resident of the state of New York.[4] Rodríguez was born in present day Santo Domingo, Dominican Republic and arrived in New York in 1613 on a Dutch merchant ship named the *Jonge Tobias,* that docked at Hudson Harbor in what is now New York City (Stevens-Acevedo, Álvarez Francés, and Weterings, 2013, 2 and Hernández and Stevens-Acevedo 2011, 473). He was a merchant who organized trade among the local people he encountered (Burrows and Wallace 1999, 19).

The notion of Dominicans as new immigrants who began to migrate en masse after the middle of the twentieth century was first challenged by renowned sociologist Ramona Hernández, director of the City University of New York's Dominican Studies Institute. Ellis Island opened on January 1, 1892—nearly two centuries after Juan Rodríguez arrived. In the first major wave of Dominican migration to the United States, between 1892 and 1924, more than five thousand Dominicans entered the country through Ellis Island (Hernández 2012, 151). Dominicans continued to migrate via that port until it closed its immigration facilities in 1954.

Participation of Dominicans in the United States military is considered a fairly new phenomenon that started during the Second World War. At that time, migrants like José Cabrera—whose interview is in the Dominican Archives at the CUNY Dominican Studies Institute—fought for the United States. However, another significant Dominican migrant often overlooked by the history books is Captain José Gabriel Luperón, older brother of former Dominican President Gregorio Luperón. According to Silvio Torres-Saillant (2000, 258), US President Abraham Lincoln awarded José Gabriel Luperón the rank of captain upon his successful participation in the Civil War. He was thus recognized by Lincoln for his decisive role in a naval battle for the Union troops (Torres-Saillant and Hernández 1998, 105).

The Intellectual History of Dominican Migration

Historically, the earliest Dominican migrants have remained invisible within the US literature regarding the fabric of its society. When Dominican migrants are acknowledged, they are viewed as "other" Hispanics or Latinos, as though there is one model, or mainstream Latino or Hispanic group. There are even times when the Spanish-speaking Caribbean islands are lumped together as part of Central America. Preeminent scholar of Dominican Studies, Silvio Torres-Saillant, was among the earliest writers to bring awareness to non-Dominicans, regarding the intellectual history of Dominican migration in the United States. According to Torres-Saillant:

> The state of knowledge about the cultural life of Dominicans in the United States is dismal. Most reference publications that purport to account for the ethnic groups that make up the American people, including those dealing specifically with the Hispanic portion of the U.S. population, leave Dominicans out. (2000, 258)

Daisy Cocco De Filippis (2011, 53) echoes Dr. Torres-Saillant when she writes, "historically, scholarship on Latinos in the U.S. has not included the literary work of Dominicans in the U.S." The groundbreaking works of Drs. Silvio Torres-Saillant, Daisy Cocco De Filippis, and Ramona Hernández, have challenged earlier scholarly claims that the first major wave of Dominican migration, or the literature produced by Dominican migrants to the United States, both began in the 1960s.

Intellectual history encompasses that of ideas, especially the documented history of the written word. Chief Librarian Sarah Aponte, preeminent bibliographer of Dominican studies and founder of the Dominican Library at the Dominican Studies Institute, has identified most of the literature produced by Dominican migrants through some of her groundbreaking works. These include her first research monograph, *Dominican Migration to the United States 1970–1997: An Annotated Bibliography*; the peer-reviewed article, "Dominican Related Dissertations in the U.S.: An Analytical Approach (1939–2009)"; and the monograph, *Autores dominicanos de la diáspora: apuntes bio-bibliográficos (1902–2012)*, which she co-authored with Franklin Gutiérrez. According to Aponte, *Cuentos frágiles* by Fabio Fiallo and *Renuevos* by José M. Bernard were the first two texts by Dominican migrants published in the United States, specifically in the City of New York, by Imprenta de H. Braeunlich and Imprenta Hispano-Americana, respectively (Aponte and Gutiérrez 2013, 10).

Dominican Periodicals

Though not all Dominican immigrants yearn for their homeland, most have traditionally maintained a connectedness. One manner in which they manifest their "Dominicanness" is by maintaining some of their attachments to the Dominican Republic. One form in which this yearning has manifested over the years is through the establishment of Dominican-owned newspapers, magazines and, nowadays, online portals such as blogs and unconventional news websites, including Remolacha.net and Esendom.com.

On the tragic day of September 11, 2001, *Dominican Times Magazine* was launched. The magazine has undergone several name changes and today is called *Latin Trends*, in order to appeal to all Hispanic/Latino groups. A decade prior to the *Dominican Times*, the newspaper *Listín USA* was founded in the early nineties. The seventies and eighties saw the largest boom in print periodicals founded by Dominican migrants. These focused exclusively on the experience or an aspect of Dominican culture, whether in the Dominican Republic or in the United States. Some of these now defunct periodicals include *Merengue*, a magazine originally named *Dominicana Ilustrada*, founded in 1979; and the newspaper *La Voz del Reformista*, founded in 1985. As evident in their names, *Merengue* and *La Voz del Reformista* allude to something Dominican. Merengue is one of the two musical genres most identified with Dominicans and the Dominican Republic (bachata is the other). Although *Merengue* includes some articles pertinent to music, most of the content pertains to different facets of Dominican society, including Dominican migrants in the United States and politics in the Dominican Republic. *La Voz del Reformista* refers to the political party known as the *Partido Reformista Social Cristiano*, founded in 1963 by Joaquín Balaguer while he was exiled in New York.

However, as noted by Torres-Saillant and Aponte, even before the formation of the aforementioned print periodicals Dominican migrants and non-migrants were publishing articles in US-based newspapers such as *Las Novedades: España y los Pueblos Hispano-Americanos*, whose roots in New York go back to 1876, and *La Prensa*, established in 1913. Dominican writers in the first two decades of the twentieth century had a strong affinity to *Las Novedades* (Torres-Saillant 2000, 262–63; Torres-Saillant and Hernández 1998, 106; Aponte and Gutiérrez 2013, 10).[5] Among many other renowned writers, Manuel de Jesús Galván, author of the *magnum opus*, *Enriquillo*, and Pedro Henríquez Ureña contributed to *Las Novedades*. Henríquez Ureña was one of the earliest Dominican migrants to earn a doctorate in the United States. He did so in 1918 at the University of Minnesota, where he also taught, and several years later he became a visiting professor at Harvard University (Torres-Saillant 2000, 106–7). In addition, between 1914 and 1918, *Las Novedades* newspaper changed ownership under two Dominicans, Francisco José Peynado and Juan Bautista Vicini Burgos (Aponte and Gutiérrez 2013, 11).[6] Vicini Burgos served as Dominican president under the United States occupation, between 1922 and 1924, while Peynado served as ambassador to the United States from 1912 to 1913.

The Great Dominican Exodus

The best known Dominican migration coincides with the dictatorship of Rafael Leónidas Trujillo and spiked after his death. According to Ernst Georg Ravenstein's push-pull theory, certain factors push people out of their homeland, forcing them to migrate elsewhere. The place these people migrate to offers them an attractive alternative. During the fifties and sixties, specific conditions forced Dominicans to migrate to the United States in record numbers: unemployment, deteriorating social conditions, a subpar quality of life and, in some cases, persecution. According to scholars such as Jesse Hofnung-Garskof (2008, 97–98) and Silvio Torres-Saillant, most of these migrants were the product of an "economic exile," meaning they were forced out due to the severe economic and social conditions in the Dominican Republic.[7]

Dictator Rafael Leónidas Trujillo ruled the Dominican Republic with an iron first for thirty-one years, from 1930 until 1961, when he was assassinated by Dominicans who were tired of his bloody reign. Like other Latin American dictators, Trujillo was initially supported by the United States after being groomed to rule by the superpower. Trujillo was manic to the point at which he built monuments in his honor. For one, he commissioned the *Monumento a la Paz de Trujillo* (Trujillo's Monument of Peace). However, upon his death the monument was rechristened *Monumento a los Héroes de la Restauración* (Monument to the Heroes of the Restoration). Due to the destruction in the aftermath of Hurricane San Zenón in 1930, Trujillo took the liberty of renaming the capital city of Santo Domingo after himself: Ciudad Trujillo. It reverted to Santo Domingo upon his death, though there are books, dissertations, and other documents that bear the name Ciudad Trujillo as the city of publication.

Trujillo's grip extended to migration, a policy in which he refused nearly every Dominican the opportunity to leave the nation. The severe restrictions his government imposed included the exorbitant cost of passports. Even worse, the government also denied passports to people who could afford to travel (Hoffnung-Garskof 2008, 70). Dominicans opposed to the dictatorship fled the nation, particularly during the fifties. However, it was not until after the death of the dictator on May 30, 1961, that Dominicans experienced migratory freedom. In fact, it was during the presidency of Trujillo's pupil, Joaquín Balaguer (1966–78), when Dominican migration escalated, especially to New York (Aparicio 2006, 55–59). This moment has become known historically as the "Great Dominican Exodus." Consequently, this also led to a boom in the intellectual history of Dominican migration in the United States. Unlike Dominicans who entered through Ellis Island, those who migrated during the presidency of Joaquín Balaguer after Trujillo's fall were mostly working-class migrants. This post-Trujillo migration also included professionals such as doctors, lawyers, and businesspeople, as well as leftists against the Dominican government and the United States.

Some of these working-class migrants founded several Dominican organizations and important networks that are still active. For instance, Juan Antonio Paulino and Normandía Maldonado are among the founders of the Club Cívico y Cultural Juan Pablo Duarte, known today as Instituto Duartiano de Estados Unidos. The organization was founded in 1966, four years after the Centro Cívico Cultural Dominicano in 1962. Normandía Maldonado was among the founders of several other organizations. In 1967, she founded the oldest continuously performing US-Dominican folkloric dance troupe: the Centro Cultural Ballet Quisqueya. Over a decade later in 1982, she, Miguel Amaro and a slew of other Dominicans founded the National Dominican Day Parade. Unlike Maldonado and Paulino, Amaro was among a group of Dominicans with some college education, having graduated the City University of New York's Brooklyn College.

Dominican-Related Dissertations

The massive wave of Dominican migration contributed to increased publication of Dominican intellectual thought. According to Aponte, of 673 Dominican-related dissertations produced in the United States between 1939 and 2009, fifty-seven pertained to an aspect of Dominican migration to the US. The first known Dominican-related dissertation published in the US was produced by Louise Jordan, an American, in 1939 for a doctoral degree in paleontology at the Massachusetts Institute of Technology (MIT). Eduardo de Latorre is the first known Dominican scholar to produce a Dominican-related dissertation, titled *The Dominican Republic: A Case Study of a Caudillistic Political System and the Challenge of a Populist Movement.* Latorre submitted it to Columbia University in 1972 to earn his PhD in political science. Between 1902 and 1960, Dominican migrants authored 72 books and between 1961 and 2012, Dominican migrants authored a total of 965 books (Aponte 2011, 13–29). In fact, from 1981 through 2012, the number of books published doubled from one decade to the next. It is important to note that some of these authors were not born in the Dominican Republic; however, they are the children of Dominican immigrants, including renowned novelist Julia Alvarez.

Conclusion

Leaving one's homeland is never an easy task. Migrants often depart with mixed feelings of melancholia and bittersweet happiness, as noted in Frank Reyes's bachata song, "Vine a decirte adios." The song became an anthem, not only for Dominicans, but for other Spanish-speaking Latin American migrants to the United States.

The intellectual history of Dominican migration is too great to compress into a single article. There are countless narratives that need to be told; for instance, about the activism of Dr. Mary Ely Gratereaux and Mercedes Cepín. In the eighties, these two women rallied Dominicans and other Hispanics/Latinos to oppose Roman Catholic priests who refused to hold mass for them in the same place as white parishioners. Instead they were forced to receive the sermon of the Lord in the church basement. They opposed this injustice and won the battle, which is documented in several New York City newspapers as well as a book written by a sympathetic Roman Catholic priest. There are also stories of countless other Dominican migrants that need telling: of the factory worker, the community organizer, the elected official, the single mother, and so forth. There is a reason why there are community organizations, streets, schools, monuments, and parks throughout the United States, named after something Dominican-related. This is because, although transplanted, Dominican migrants and their descendants have contributed much to the place they will forever call home.

NOTES

1. A *barahonera* is a girl or woman from the Dominican province of Barahona.

2. In addition to Linares in New York, in 1991 Kay Palacios was elected to the New Jersey City Council, yet her name is many times unjustly omitted from the conversation.

3. *La ciguapa* is a female character in Dominican mythology. She is characterized by her backward feet and is known to bewitch men.

4. Anthony Stevens-Acevedo is the first researcher to emphasize the significance of Juan Rodríguez's arrival.

5. Sarah Aponte has presented on *Las Novedades* at several conferences and is currently preparing a manuscript relating to this invaluable periodical.

6. Please note that some previous scholarship erroneously lists Peynado and Vicini Burgos as founders of *Las Novedades*.

7. Hoffnung-Garskof explains that Dominicans saw themselves as "economic exiles" who escaped from the misery and unemployment created by the Dominican government.

REFERENCES

Aparicio, Ana. 2006. *Dominican-Americans and the Politics of Empowerment*. Gainesville: University Press of Florida.

Aponte, Sarah. 1999. *Dominican Migration to the United States, 1970–1997: An Annotated Bibliography*. New York: CUNY Dominican Studies Institute.

———. 2011. "Dominican Related Dissertations in the U.S.: An Analytical Approach (1939–2009)." *Camino Real: Estudios de las Hispanidades Norteamericanas* 3 (4): 21–51.

Aponte, Sarah, and Franklin Gutiérrez. 2013. *Autores dominicanos de la diáspora: apuntes bio-bibliográficos (1902–2012)*. Santo Domingo: Biblioteca Nacional Pedro Henríquez Ureña.

Bernard, José. 1908. *Renuevos*. New York: Imprenta Hispano-Americana.

Burrows, Edwin G., and Mike Wallace. 1999. *Gotham: A History of New York City to 1898*. New York: Oxford University Press.

Cocco De Filippis, Daisy. 2011. "Las tertulias de las escritoras dominicanas en Estados Unidos: una historia." *Camino Real: Estudios de las Hispanidades Norteamericanas* 3 (4): 53–71.

Díaz, Junot. 2007. *The Brief Wondrous Life of Oscar Wao*. New York: Riverhead Books.

Fiallo, Fabio. 1908. *Cuentos frágiles*. New York: Imprenta de H. Braeunlich.

Hernández, Ramona. 2012. "The Dominican American Family." In *Ethnic Families in America: Patterns and Variations*, 5th ed., edited by Roosevelt H. Wright Jr., Robert W. Habenstein, Charles H. Mindel, and Thanh Van Tran, 148–73. Boston: Pearson.

Hernández, Ramona and Anthony Stevens-Acevedo. 2011. "Dominican Immigrants." In Vol. 1 of *Multicultural America: An Encyclopedia of the Newest Americans*, edited by Ron Bayor, 471–532. Santa Barbara: Greenwood.

Hoffnung-Garskof, Jesse. 2008. *A Tale of Two Cities: Santo Domingo and New York After 1950*. Princeton: Princeton University Press.

Lowe, John. 1998. "Juan Marichal: He Was Winningest Pitcher of '60s." *Baseball Digest* 57 (8): 74.

Moore, Robin, and Walter Aaron Clark, eds. 2012. *Musics of Latin America*. New York: Norton.

O'Gorman, Edmundo. 1958. *La invención de América: El universalismo de la cultura de Occidente*. México: Fondo de Cultura Económico.

Reyes, Frank. 1998. "Vine a decirte adiós." *Vine a decirte adiós*. J & N Records, CD.

Stevens-Acevedo, Anthony, Leonor Álvarez Francés, and Tom Weterings. 2013. *Juan Rodríguez and the Beginnings of New York City*. New York: CUNY Dominican Studies Institute.

Torres-Saillant, Silvio. 2000. "Before the Diaspora: Early Dominican Literature in the United States." In Vol. 3 of *Recovering the U.S. Hispanic Literary Heritage*, edited by María Herrera-Sobek and Virginia Sánchez Korrol, 250–67. Houston: Arte Público.

Torres-Saillant, Silvio, and Ramona Hernández. 1998. *The Dominican Americans*. Westport: Greenwood.

7. Identity Politics and Puerto Rican Visual Resources

María del Mar González-González

This paper will focus on my experience conducting research in archives of Puerto Rican visual arts and culture. My nearly eight years of this research have been conducted in both public and private archives in Puerto Rico, New York, Washington, DC, and Los Angeles. I will mainly discuss my work on the Island and will expand upon other locations if time permits. During the years that I have been conducting research in and about Puerto Rico, I have had the opportunity to visit both public and private archives. Among those that I have consulted on the Island are: the Colección de las Artes and Colección Puertorriqueña, both at the Biblioteca José M. Lázaro at the Universidad de Puerto Rico, Recinto de Río Piedras; the archives at the Museo de Arte, Historia, Antropología y Arte, also on that campus; the library of the Centro de Estudios Avanzados de Puerto Rico y el Caribe; the institutional archive of the División de Artes Plásticas of the Instituto de Cultura Puertorriqueña; the Revista del Instituto de Cultura Puertorriqueña; the Archivo General de Puerto Rico; the Museo Pío López at the Universidad de Puerto Rico en Cayey; la Fundación Luis Muñoz Marín; and the private archives of art historian Margarita Fernández Zavala, artist Antonio Martorell, and art historian Teresa Tió.

As stated previously, in the continental US I have consulted archives primarily in New York City and Washington, DC, and somewhat less successfully in Los Angeles. In New York, I mostly focused on The Museum Archives, Museum of Modern Art and the Centro de Estudios Puertorriqueños, Hunter College, City University of New York. While in Washington, I worked at the Archives Center at the National Museum of American History; the Smithsonian Institute Archives of American Art, the Smithsonian Institution; and the Library of Congress. In Los Angeles, I worked at the archives at the Getty Research Institute and the Chicano Studies Research Center at UCLA.

Although every institution has been different, Puerto Rico's colonial status vis-à-vis the United States and the friction that this creates take quite a toll on collecting practices for both Puerto Rican art and document archives, both

Who Are We Really?: Latin American Family, Local and Micro-Regional Histories, and Their Impact on Understanding Ourselves. Papers of the Fifty-Ninth Annual Meeting of SALALM, 2014.

on and outside the Island. Several socioeconomic factors have come together to create this. One is the Island's dual political and economic dependence on the US. Many wish it were finally resolved in the form of independence or statehood, as it leads to much conflict among locals with polarized political affiliations. This, in turn, leads to internal political tensions and economic constraints. Why would this affect archives? The majority of Island archives are government sponsored. Given political tensions, depending on which of the two main political parties is in power, arts and cultural institutions face obstacles to access the materials in most local, government-funded archives. Among those obstacles are politically appointed directors who might not have the interest or credentials. Others are severe budget cuts that lead to shortages influencing staffing, organization, operating hours, acquisition of materials, and preservation, to just name a few.

These political tensions are often exacerbated when combined with the larger, global economic crisis that we've faced this past decade. This led to the economic crisis of 2006 when the Puerto Rican governor, Aníbal Acevedo Vilá, and the local legislature were unable to reach a budget agreement, the state government had to close down that May due to a lack of funds, and there were threats that it might happen again in 2010 and 2011. This led to a complete halt of activity on the Island, not only in the government shutdown but also in the closing of public schools, which put almost one hundred thousand people out of work temporarily. As a personal example, this was during the summer that I was going to conduct my first pre-dissertation trip. I had received a research travel grant and had all of my arrangements made, only to find out a few weeks before that I would very likely not be able to conduct research. In the end it worked out.

The economy of Puerto Rico has continued to languish. Among the outcomes of the weakened economy was the slashing of state funding for the state university and, in 2010, the governor mandated a hike in student tuition, which included a special quota added to the Universidad de Puerto Rico system. These increases were met with student protests, and countered by then-governor Luis Fortuño with the state police's occupation of the Rio Piedras campus in 2010 and 2011.

As you can imagine, conducting research on the Island has been far from easy. The archives that I consulted there operate with various degrees of stability. What I have encountered during my research trips is that visual art and cultural resources in Puerto Rico tend to be fragile and incomplete, fragmented and divided among various locations without much rhyme or reason, and neglected in terms of organization and preservation. There have been some isolated efforts to collect and preserve often delicate and ephemeral materials that can tell us about local artistic production, exhibition and curatorial practices, and critical reception, as well as the participation of Island artists in national and international arenas.

Despite these issues, visual arts production in Puerto Rico has had a fairly robust run, especially during the postwar boom. Various art museums, artists' workshops, galleries, and cultural institutions, such as the Instituto de Cultura Puertorriqueña, established in 1955, were developed to support and showcase artistic production. However, its materials—like exhibition files; artwork catalogs; and ephemera such as manifestos, flyers, memos, and agendas—have not been preserved. Given the economic constraints of most of these institutions, the fleeting nature of most of the organizations and events, and perhaps even due to a lack of foresight, most of these institutions have prioritized the hosting of active exhibition programs over preserving records of the artists' work. Moreover, many of these short-lived artists' organizations never had a physical location, but met on a rotating basis at different places and pooled funds to rent out exhibition spaces. This leads to a crucial question: Where might the records have been preserved when the organizations themselves were nomadic? Without such a repository or series of them, vital materials that would have added depth and dimension to the history of art in Puerto Rico have been lost or dispersed, along with most of the institutional memory about their events and rotating locations. This also goes for the precious few such materials that remain.

Despite several local efforts, many artists' and institutional archives remain lost or are disorganized, and I fear that they teeter on the verge of perishing. Most of these histories are preserved in the form of memories, which could be rescued as oral histories. However, the Instituto de Cultura Puertorriqueña, or ICP for short, was created under Law 89 of 1955 by the Commonwealth government in power at the time. It was and remains responsible for the establishment of cultural policies in order to "preserve, promote, research and divulge the Puerto Rican culture in its complex diversity."[1] The ICP has several subdivisions to enact its purpose of preserving local history and culture. These divisions have documented the history of Puerto Rico's art and culture since the mid 1950s through the accumulation of separate but related collections of materials. Today I will address my experiences at the División de Artes Plásticas, established in 1973, and at the Archivo General de Puerto Rico, established in 1955. Given that the subject and object of my research is the San Juan Print Biennial, held from 1969 through the present and organized by the ICP, I have spent many hours in various Instituto archives. The Biennial's office and archives have been housed at the División de Artes Plásticas since the division's creation in 1973. For that reason, I visit its offices quite frequently. When I first visited the Artes Plásticas's so-called "archive" in 2006, I was surprised to find they did not have an archivist in charge of these materials, nor was any other person in charge of maintaining or managing the archive. Instead, the various staff people, completely untrained in archiving, much less preserving, took turns assisting visiting researchers.

These conditions led to the lack of an actual system with which to organize its files. Those that I needed to consult were on the first floor, in the makeshift file room of a beautiful yet leaky colonial building on the bay of San Juan. One can just imagine the humidity issues they face! In addition to the documents such as exhibition files and catalogs, and ephemera such as memos, checklists, and agendas, Artes Plásticas is also supposed to own and manage the collection of the Biennial's winning prints. Yet, when I requested the artwork, much to my dismay, none of the employees knew the location of these prints, nor could they find documentation that they existed. As an art historian interested in visual production, these prints are a crucial portion of my research. I have summarized the problems with their archival management into a few points:

1. Management and arrangement: There was no management or organization of the records or materials, no record of which documents were kept or where they were located within the archive.

2. Access: Virtually anyone could walk in, sort through the archives, and misfile or take what they wanted from the piled boxes.

3. Physical state: The documents were in various stages of neglect, stored in high-risk, non-archival conditions. Specifically, they were kept in a humid, mold- and mildew-prone space, which will not only lead to their destruction, but poses a health hazard to those who come into contact with them. Years of water damage and mishandling of the documents made my work at Artes Plásticas quite an adventure and required the use of safety gear, such as gloves, a mask, and protective eye wear.

4. Lack of institutional memory: There was little continuity in record keeping or organizational structure. On the institutional level, this led to a fragile and fragmented history of the Instituto de Cultura Puertorriqueña.

Another of my research locations was the Archivo General de Puerto Rico, founded in 1955 and in its current location since 1977. It is also managed by the Instituto de Cultura Puertorriqueña and is composed of five units. It's responsible for preserving public documents of historical importance for the Island and is the largest repository of its historic documents. Access to the Archivo General is more restricted than in most archives in Puerto Rico. It requires an interview and letter of introduction explaining the purpose of one's visit.

The Archivo General has a team of trained archivists who assist visiting researchers. Given that the stacks and file room are closed, one is required to fill out a form indicating which boxes will be used, and these are limited to three per request form. The first time I visited the Archivo General in 2006, I was surprised at its stark contrast with Artes Plásticas. There were cataloged binders neatly organized chronologically by the government office to which the documents had belonged. I was thrilled.

The problem, however, became quickly apparent once I began requesting boxes. I realized that the box numbers and allegedly chronologically arranged contents did not correspond with each other. Although most of the boxes did correspond to the government agency—the ICP—the contents did not follow any kind of rational organization. After much confusion, I set out to find an archivist to help me decipher the system. She then admitted that the arts were not an archival priority, and that the boxes were in the same state and order as when they were sent to the Archivo back in the 1970s. Despite my profound disappointment and difficulties in the archive, the majority of archivists with whom I interacted were extremely helpful. One of them, against protocol, even allowed me in the back with her to search through the disorganized document boxes.

As the national repository of government and national governments, the Archivo faces severe challenges. Even though it seemed organized at first, and was staffed by a trained group of archivists, it has been plagued by severe budget cuts, constant changes in leadership, and shutdown threats. These occur almost every time the Island's government changes and are more or less severe depending on the incumbent governor's agenda. These shortages and administrative changes impact productivity and the institution's profile, including a range of concerns, from whether the archive should even remain open, to which documents merit priority over others. Moreover, the lack of organization of ICP documents shows that arts and cultural archives are not a priority within the institution that, ironically, should study, preserve, diffuse, and enrich Puerto Rican national culture and values. These are problems that sadly plague most government-funded cultural institutions.

I will add that this archive is incredibly difficult to access during the summer and winter break periods, the actual moments in which most of us academics can set aside time for research. On several occasions, I tried contacting a specific division director via phone and e-mail and never received a response. I realized that in addition to the abundant holidays on the Island during the summer and winter, staff coordination was not the archive's forte. When I attempted to schedule an appointment in one of their units, I was told that the archivist and her assistant had both left for vacation during the same dates and for the entire summer. Thus this unit was left closed and unstaffed for requests for the months of June and July.

However, not all has been bad. One of the most organized archives that I have worked in was that of the library at the Centro de Estudios Avanzados de Puerto Rico y el Caribe. The Centro de Estudios is a private institution for research and higher education. It became an academic institution in 1976 under the leadership of archeologist, anthropologist, and historian Ricardo Alegría, who was also the founding director of the Instituto Cultural Puertorriqueña. This is one example that shows how tightly everything is connected in Puerto Rico, for most of the archives reflect back to Alegría's work and to one of the political parties of the 1950s.

The library of the Centro houses a small, immaculately organized archive of many of Alegría's documents dating back to his years as director of the ICP. Ironically, it was here I was able to access ICP documents, such as press releases and correspondence between Alegría and other intellectuals connected to the US Congress and US art collections. Such correspondence, as with the Library of Congress and the Museum of Modern Art in New York, was not available in any of the various institutional archives of the ICP. As organized and crucial as this archive was to my work, it showed fragmentation of its historical materials and lack of communication among archives. It further points to the problem that the ICP does not recognize the historical value of its own institution. It thus fails to accurately archive or document its own production: exhibition catalogs, newsletters, and other ephemera related to their operations and activities. The findings at the Centro helped me fill in gaps in the research I conducted at previous institutions. Even so, I am still troubled by the fact that one such as the Instituto de Cultura Puertorriqueña, which preserves the Island's cultural patrimony, does not have a developed organizational structure. It is also disturbing that most of its employees, who are political appointees, seem indifferent towards the purpose and mission of archives and libraries.

The state university, the Universidad de Puerto Rico (UPR), Recinto de Río Piedras, houses several important collections. The Colección Puertorriqueña and Colección de las Artes are both at the Biblioteca José M. Lázaro, and there is also an archive at the Museo de Historia, Antropología y Arte de Río Piedras. All three are wonderful resources for rare documents and ephemera. Yet, as part of the state university, they are also haunted by local government problems. Like all government-funded cultural institutions, their budgets are constantly under threat and diminishing, while fairly constant administrative changes at the presidential and rectorial level make productivity all-around unstable. Although many employees are apathetic and seem to only be there for a paycheck, there are indeed some amazing librarians and archivists who work with incredibly meager budgets and a limited staff and somehow make them work.

Mentioned above, the art museum at UPR, Río Piedras's Museo de Historia, Antropología y Arte is noteworthy. Housed in a leaky, mid-century modern building near the campus's main entrance, this tiny institution runs on a shoestring budget with a mostly part-time staff. Aware of many of the aforementioned political and economic problems, the museum's director, Flavia Marichal, has implemented a modest system to ensure the preservation of an archive on modern and contemporary art in Puerto Rico. The director herself is a vast resource of knowledge because she grew up in the midst of the post-war Puerto Rican art boom and is the daughter of an influential printmaker, Spanish exile Carlos Marichal. However, despite her efforts, there is virtually no institutional support and the museum facilities are falling apart. Due to limited staffing, it is also difficult to access the archive from afar. One must be on the premises in order to consult their catalog, given that they haven't the budget to digitize it.

I've also been able to access a few private archives of mostly art historians and artists, though I've been denied access to others by their families. Given their private nature, these archives vary in content, but all include materials that add detail and texture to the histories of visual culture in Puerto Rico. The selection of newspaper clippings, drafts, letters, and other ephemera that I encountered usually documented moments of conflict that were virtually forgotten or selectively omitted from institutional archives. Although not as extensive as the government-funded archives, for obvious reasons such as funding and space, these private collections have been meaningful to my understanding of Puerto Rico's art and cultural history, nonetheless. In addition, though oral histories are sometimes forgotten in such research, those I gathered while working in the homes of various artists and curators have been invaluable. Together, they add to a better understanding of local artistic production, exhibition practices, and critical reception, among other things. Yet, I wonder what will happen to these archives once their owners pass away? Will they be discarded or will their inheritors acknowledge their value and either keep them or give them to a repository?

The overall lack of conscientiousness I've discussed is indeed regrettable and inexcusable. I have a few suggestions as to how to get back on track before it's too late, these archives deteriorate, and opportunities to acquire or expand collections disappear. Before I delve into those ideas, an infamous example was Teodoro Vidal's collection. The Vidal Collection is considered the most comprehensive set of holdings of Puerto Rican material culture from the seventeenth through twentieth centuries. Due to political and economic constraints, this collection was donated to the Smithsonian National Museum of American History instead of being kept at a local institution. Scholars still lament the loss of national patrimony, which should have remained on the Island.

Losses such as that of the Vidal Collection show us that we need to begin by cultivating a respect for history and national patrimony, not only among academics and archivists, but in everyone, especially politicians. This collective amnesia about the Island's history can still be remedied through collective efforts. In order to battle institutionalized ignorance we need to increase awareness and knowledge of archival practices, to reach beyond the archivists and researchers who use their collections and services. There should also be coordination and cooperation among local archives. Finally, I recommend conducting a survey of existing resources, collections and initiatives, and ideally making it available through a website or wiki page that features at least an index or table of contents.

A shift in increasing awareness and interest in Latino/a and Latin American art in the continental US has created a forum or model that Puerto Rico can either join or follow, respectively. Due to its access, one the most successful and best known of these is the International Center for the Arts of the Americas (ICAA) at the Museum of Fine Arts in Houston (MFAH). This multiyear, multi-institutional, digital archiving project, titled "Documents of 20th Century Latin American and Latino Art," is led by MFAH Curator of Latin American Art, Mari Carmen Ramirez. Its primary goal is to "provide access to primary sources and critical documents tracing the development of twentieth-century art in Latin America and among Latino populations in the United States." Ramirez's team has been collaborating with other professionals throughout Latin America and the US to build this archive. The majority of this project has been funded by soft money grants and receives institutional support from the MFAH. The ICAA and other projects in the continental US— such as the Smithsonian Institution's Archives of American Art, the Museum of Modern Art Library in New York, and the Chicano Studies Research Center at the University of California, Los Angeles—have helped increase awareness of and access to research materials and collections. Not only have they made crucial recovery efforts to document the arts, but they provide useful resources on the production of Latin American and Latino visual culture to scholars, researchers, and the community at large.

Though on a much smaller scale, another positive development comes from a small group of us, including art historians, artists, and archivists. We have been meeting via Skype both to create a network and comprise a list of young art historians, archivists, critics, and artists that either work in or conduct research on Puerto Rico. The idea is to create a digital bibliography and visual resources depository that will pool work and facilitate access to materials in order to encourage research, curatorial projects, and collaboration.

NOTE

1. The bill drafted by Governor Muñoz Marín was filed in the House of Representatives by Ernesto Ramos Antonini (PPD), president of the body, and defended by Representative Jorge Font-Saldaña (PPD). See the ICP website (http://www.icp.gobierno.pr/quiene-somos/acerca-del-icp) for basic information on their mission and history. For a detailed history, see Alegría (1996, 7–9, 257–260). See also Dávila (1997, 39); Flores Collazo (1998); Hernández (2002, 160); Benítez (1988, 83); Maldonado (2006, 352–53); and *Debates* (1955).

REFERENCES

Alegría, Ricardo. 1996. *El Instituto de Cultura Puertorriqueña 1955–1973: 18 años contribuyendo a fortalecer nuestra conciencia nacional.* Barcelona: Instituto de Cultura Puertorriqueña.

Benítez, Marimar. 1988. "The Special Case of Puerto Rico." In *The Latin American Spirit: Art and Artists in the United States, 1920–1970,* edited by Luis Cancel. New York: Harry N. Abrams.

Dávila, Arlene M. 1997. *Sponsored Identities: Cultural Politics in Puerto Rico.* Philadelphia: Temple University Press.

"Debates: Cámara vota por Instituto de Cultura." 1955. *El Mundo,* May 18.

Flores Collazo, Margarita. 1998. "La lucha por definir la nación: el debate en torno a la creación del Instituto de Cultura Puertorriqueña, 1955." *Op. Cit.: Revista del Centro de Investigaciones Históricas* 10: 175–99.

Hernández, Carmen Dolores. 2002. *Ricardo Alegría: una vida.* San Juan: Editorial Plaza Mayor.

Maldonado, A. W. 2006. *Luis Muñoz Marín: Puerto Rico's Democratic Revolution.* San Juan: La Editorial, Universidad de Puerto Rico.

8. Challenges and Alternatives to Caribbean Family History and Genealogy: Archives and Sources in Puerto Rico

Antonio Sotomayor

Family history and genealogy has experienced a boom in recent years. Websites like Ancestry.com, Familysearch.org, Geni.com, and Geneanet.org have grown both in content and membership to levels never seen before. The genealogy frenzy has reached television with shows like *Who Do You Think You Are?* (BBC in the UK and NBC/TLC in the US) and *Finding Your Roots* with Henry Louis Gates, Jr. on PBS. The study of families, lineages, and ancestral backgrounds has even entered in cutting-edge scientific disciplines such as molecular anthropology and genetics, popularly known as genetic genealogy. Genetic genealogy has proven to be highly attractive to individuals who have come across a "brick wall," or who have run out of documentary sources to trace their families further into the past (Fitzpatrick and Yeiser 2005; Pomery 2007; El-Haj 2007; Larmuseau, Van Geystelen, and Van Oven 2013).

Genetic genealogy has claimed special success in helping break down those brick walls. Although the tradition of "family names" in the Western World has been in place since the eleventh and twelve centuries, few people can actually trace their families back to those times, unless of noble ancestry or a public role in society. Yet most people can trace their ancestors back to the eighteenth century in societies with good record keeping. This is the case in many Latin American countries, where there has been a long tradition in tracing family lineages. As early as the sixteenth century, for example, colonists of Peru sought to gain social prestige by documenting their families to the conquistadors (Lockhart 1994, 191). This emphasis on Spanish family history has associated genealogy research with lineage adulation. On the other hand, searches to trace family histories of enslaved or indigenous peoples face insurmountable difficulties due to subaltern positions of their descendants. Recently there has been a shift in genealogy towards democratization, and many people look to genealogy to learn about their families without a need to find aristocratic ancestors.

Who Are We Really?: Latin American Family, Local and Micro-Regional Histories, and Their Impact on Understanding Ourselves. Papers of the Fifty-Ninth Annual Meeting of SALALM, 2014.

The Spanish Empire is known to have kept good administrative written records. While this is beneficial for economic, political, and sociohistorical research, we are only beginning to understand how this translates into the genealogical. Yet access to these records is still difficult. For the peripheral areas of what was once the empire, such as Puerto Rico and other parts of the Caribbean, resources are scarce and limited, at least for the first two and a half centuries of Spanish colonization, the early 1500s to the 1750s. Moreover, much of the documentation with potential for genealogists still resides in Spanish archives or elsewhere. After the second half of the eighteenth century we have more local records and by the nineteenth century, more and better resources become available.

This article will discuss the challenges to doing genealogical research in the Spanish Caribbean, particularly in Puerto Rico, and will sporadically use the Sotomayor family as an example. It will also discuss alternatives for the researcher to address these challenges. In doing so, it will present the current state of the field of genealogy on the Island and its diaspora. The article will discuss some of the traditional genealogical works, then specific challenges to researching genealogy. Finally, it will introduce ways of overcoming the limitations to deep genealogical research, including the importance of historical context and DNA testing.

Puerto Rican Genealogies

Puerto Ricans have been researching and publishing genealogical work for most of the twentieth century. One of the earliest works is Enrique Ramírez Brau's (1947) *Orígenes puertorriqueños*. This is a very well researched volume that provides a narrative history of the Ramírez de Arellano family and its descendants. It also provides abbreviated information on various birth, marriage, and death records of its members, covering the mid- to late-seventeenth century to the mid-nineteenth century. The benefits of this volume are its chronological coverage and its inclusion of other families. That is, while it focuses on the Ramírez de Arellano family it also includes other families that married into it.

Similar to Ramírez Brau's book is Francisco Lluch Mora's (1976) *Catálogo de inscripciones demográfico-sacramentales y de otra índole del linaje puertorriqueño Ortiz de la Renta*. Lluch Mora provides valuable information on the sixteenth century ancestry of the Ortiz de la Renta lineage in Puerto Rico, mainly in western towns, and the families it married into. He then lists sacramental records for each town as far back as records exist. For the Colón family in Puerto Rico, associated with Cristóbal Colón, there is Edmund Colón's (1988) *Colón Families of the Seventeenth Century in Puerto Rico*. This is a valuable book, although the recent research on the Colón family by Gil-Loyzaga (2007) is also recommended. Another important volume is Martín Gaudier's (1963–64) *Genealogías puertorriqueñas*. Although this book does not focus on one family, hence does not analyze deep ancestry, it does list as many genealogies from as many towns on the Island as possible. There is an index that the user may consult directly for specific surnames and dates. There are many more books on Puerto Rican genealogies, often focusing on certain wealthy families, particular towns, or time periods. They range from documentary information to micro-histories (Acosta and Cuesta Camacho 1983; Armstrong Mejía de Blila and Villares Armstrong 2000; Barragán Landa 1996; Casanova 1982; Cuesta Camacho and Pérez Coma n.d.; Castro and Castro 1991; Dávila 1995; Delgado Plasencia 1998, 2009; Encarnación Navarro 2005; Font 1987; Gil-Loyzaga 2007; Huerga 2008, 2009; Machado Martínez 1999; Martínez Nazario 2004a, 2004b; Mayoral Barnés 1946; Negroni 1998; Nieves Méndez 2004; Platt 1990; Oquendo Pabón 2000; Reed and Kaus 1994; Rosado 1994; Sáez 1995; Santiago Torres 1986; Schmal 1994; Solivan de Acosta 1988, 1993, 1996).

Recently, family history and genealogy have been studied by professional academic historians. Among them is George Ryskamp who has had a long career as an historian at Brigham Young University, publishing academic work on Spanish and Latin American family history and anthroponymy, the study of family names (Ryskamp 2000, 2002, 2003, 2005). For the Caribbean in general and Puerto Rico specifically, the best known is David Stark, an associate professor of history at Grand Valley State University in Michigan. Aside from the white Puerto Rican population, Stark has been devoted to studying the lives and family relationships of the enslaved black population. His articles, "Parish Registers as a Window to the Past: Reconstructing the Demographic Behavior of the Enslaved Population in Eighteenth-Century Arecibo, Puerto Rico," and "The Family Tree Is Not Cut: Marriage among Slaves in Eighteenth-Century Puerto Rico," are premier examples of this type of scholarship (Stark 2002, 2006).

In his work, David Stark provides us with a much-needed window to the histories of the enslaved or blacks in colonial Latin America and the Caribbean, a severely neglected topic of research. This is because family histories and genealogies traditionally focused on elite white urban men. While researchers in the late twentieth century paid more attention to analyzing how family structures intersected with bigger social, political, and economic dynamics (Borges 1992), earlier genealogical writings focused on discovering famous or important male ancestors, extracting data on wealthy men in urban centers. Females, especially those of lower classes and rural areas, were for the most part ignored. This lack of attention to subaltern groups should not surprise us, as the field of history in general also focused on telling the stories of white elite men and their great deeds. While Puerto Rican genealogy research as a whole is still far from the study of subaltern families, the increasing number of casual researchers will only help to grow the data and family trees of the common family.

Genealogy Research in Puerto Rico: Challenges

If it is difficult to research genealogy on Puerto Rican subaltern groups, such as blacks and women, similar research is also a challenge regarding rural men. This is the case of families in the northwest of the Island where my family is from. I have been doing genealogical research for more than ten years and have visited and researched at parish, municipal, and state archives. Information on several of the branches on my family tree, both from the paternal and maternal sides, disappears around the mid-1700s and some even in the mid-1800s. While there were documented *mulata* ancestors, most of my family belonged to the rural white landowning class. In my experience, researching the past of my female ancestors, and of the mulata line, has been very difficult and I can only trace it back to the mid-1800s. As for the rest of the branches, even of the white landowning class, I can only trace them back to the mid-1700s. Here is where I hit numerous brick walls. My case is not that different from other genealogists on the Island and the following discussion will illustrate the difficulties many other researchers face when doing genealogy work in Puerto Rico.

To briefly discuss the challenges to the Sotomayor branch of my family tree, I can trace my paternal ancestry to Don Juan de Sotomayor Hernández, circa 1700, in the town of Aguada, Puerto Rico. This gentleman married Doña Rosa Lorenzo de Acevedo and they are believed to be the parents of my fifth great grandfather, Don Juan de Sotomayor. Yet, the information we have for the first Juan is fuzzy and actually comes from a secondary source.

Genealogist Rafael Reichard Sapia gathered the information and reached this conclusion after doing extensive research in the parishes of the northwest of Puerto Rico, including the towns of Moca and San Sebastián where many of my ancestors came from. Reichard Sapia found Juan de Sotomayor Hernández's death record in the parish of Moca, which stated that he died on March 6, 1791 at the age of 112 years. The problems with this record are various for genealogy. First, even though it is plausible, living for 112 years seems rather long for any human being. Although my second great grandfather died at 94 and my great aunt at 96, 112 pushes the limit! Centuries ago, even early in the twentieth century, people did not keep track of their birthdates so their ages at death were estimated. Second, we cannot find the original record anymore. When I went to look for the record in person, the archivist vehemently affirmed that the church *never* kept death records, when we know for a fact they did. Third, the record does not list Juan's parents, something not uncommon before the eighteenth and even nineteenth centuries. Fourth, although the record lists a "Juan" as one of his sons, there is no way to prove that Juan (the son) was actually my fifth great grandfather. However, the record created by Reichard Sapia in approximately the 1920s is the only source that we have for now.

Finally, my family's surname in numerous records throughout Spanish colonial times appears in different versions that include Sotomayor, Soto, Soto Mayor, Soto maior, Soto=mayor, and Soutomayor. This is because names, and grammar overall, were not standardized or as strict as they are today. The *Real Academia de la Lengua Española* was established in 1713 and started creating grammar rules in 1741, which were gradually adopted in the Americas afterwards. The first dictionary was published in 1781 (García de la Concha 2014). This inconsistency in grammar did not only occur in Puerto Rico but throughout the Spanish world, including medieval Galicia where the Sotomayors were originally from. In Galician, the name is spelled Soutomaior (Vila 2010). Other families, especially those with compound last names, experience the same situation. The name Lorenzo de Acevedo appears as Lorenzo, Lorenzo Acevedo, or Acevedo; Vélez Borrero as Vélez; Luciano de Fuentes as Luciano or Fuentes; and Ortiz de la Renta as Ortiz.

Parish archives, as the official place where birth, marriage, and death events were recorded in Latin America, constitute the first research option for genealogists. The example of my sixth great grandfather introduces us to many of the challenges genealogists face when trying to do family history in Puerto Rico's parochial archives. First, many parochial archives only have records back to the late eighteenth century, if not the early nineteenth century (Rodríguez León 1983). The town of Moca's oldest book is its First Book of Marriages, from 1775 to 1782. Moca was established in 1772 and seceded from Aguada. Although Juan de Sotomayor Hernández is said to be from the town of Aguada, its parish records only go back to 1804 (*Libro de Bautizos de Pardos*), even though the town was founded in 1648 (Nieves Acevedo 2009, 55). Another hurdle that grows more and more stringent is that researchers need to obtain special permission from the diocese's bishop in order to gain access to the archive. This is because the Catholic Church distrusts the growing genealogical work done in Latin America by the Church of Jesus Christ of the Latter Day Saints (aka Mormons). There is a formal application process and it could take months to receive a response, which could likely be a denial of access.

If the researcher gets access to the archive, another challenge is to bypass the archivist. In the best of cases, an archivist will feel overprotective of old delicate records and might pull books from public access. In the worst of cases, unscrupulous archivists or researchers steal documents or entire boxes of them, to sell on the black market. Other people might hide a document or even cross out information that would reveal sensitive information, such as illegitimacy, race, or conflicting evidence. The problem of record availability, theft, or destruction is by no means a contemporary one. For centuries, these parish archives have been suffering from a tropical climate that destroyed fragile documents. Mold, flooding, earthquakes, and ink burn are some of the natural elements that have severely affected Puerto Rican parish and civil archives, especially those of the sixteenth, seventeenth, and eighteenth centuries. Additionally, the fact that Puerto Rico is located in the Caribbean, a region characterized by constant warfare between European empires, indigenous attacks, and slave rebellions, means that many archives were lost during battles through arson, bombings, or theft.

If the documents have survived centuries of hurricanes, earthquakes, war, humidity, ink burn, and theft, the researcher might face another problem: the lack of organization and bad cataloging. Often these books are located near workspaces or hidden in boxes in separate rooms. They are at risk of being misplaced or shelved in the wrong place. They have no systematic numbering, only dates. Access to these archives is extremely limited to working hours at best, or a few days a week at worst. Some of them, particularly the General Archive in San Juan, close often due to recurring water leaks, maintenance, or air conditioning failure. At the General Archive, where the researcher finds notarial records, wills, and other civil data along with genealogical information, gaining access to boxes is extremely bureaucratic. The researcher must ask for only three boxes twice a week and can only view them after one p.m. the next day. If these boxes don't have much data and the review lasts an hour, you will have waited a full day and a half to find out.

Genealogy Research in Puerto Rico: Alternatives

Although challenges to genealogy in Puerto Rico seem cumbersome, there are several alternatives that range from online databases to DNA testing. A good website with introductory recommendations for genealogical research is *Puerto Rico en breve*, at http://www.preb.com/ref/geneal.htm. Genealogists distinguish between recent genealogy and deep genealogy. Recent genealogy researches the twentieth, nineteenth, and the late eighteenth centuries. I have chosen these centuries because there are more records available, and because they mark the stabilization of last names in the Spanish world. Although in Peninsular and New World Spanish cultures, the tradition of inheriting surnames favored the father's, a child might also inherit the mother's family name. This is because Spanish culture had a more comprehensive view of the family (Ryskamp 2005, 361–63), and while names were passed down through their fathers in 80 percent of the cases, children would also inherit their last names from their mothers, or other ancestors (Ryskamp 2005, 353). After the 1700s, when patrilineal family name inheritance became law, families consistently passed down the fathers' surnames but that was still in the era researchers consider deep genealogy. The practice of having two surnames in the Spanish world only became standard in the nineteenth century.

For recent genealogy, users can become a member of the Ancestry.com website to make use of its census data and other digitized documents. For Puerto Rico, users have access to the censuses of 1910, 1920, 1930, and 1940.

Another useful database is Familysearch.org, a part of the Church of Jesus Christ of the Latter Day Saints, which has digitized the records for Puerto Rico's civil registry and some parish records dating back to 1645. Yet the bulk of their collection is the civil registry, which was established for all of Spain and its colonies in 1885. The records in Familysearch.org for Puerto Rico are not indexed, so the user must browse record by record through 4,792,160 unindexed records and 12,475 indexed records, as of August 2014. Some of the books have indexes, and the site has saved some genealogies by other members, as does Ancestry.com, which users are encouraged to check first.

An important collection of court cases from the district of Arecibo, including the towns of Arecibo, Barceloneta, Camuy, Ciales, Hatillo, Manatí, Morovis, Quebradillas, and Utuado, cover the years between 1844 and 1900. The digital versions are held at the University of Connecticut at http://www .crl.edu/focus/article/8565, and may be accessed from that page or directly, at https://archive.org/details/puertoricancivilcourtdocuments.

Another important digital collection, one that bridges recent and deep genealogy, is the *Padrones de Puerto Rico, 1779 to 1802*. This collection gathers twenty-three censuses, covers the entire island, and provides population statistics on social status, race, and sex. The collection can be accessed, but only by the members of the Inter-University Consortium for Political and Social Research (ICPSR), part of the Institute for Social Research at the University of Michigan (http://www.icpsr.umich.edu/icpsrweb/ICPSR/studies/30262).

In addition to these databases, there are different online social groups and forums that serve as discussion sites for people looking for research hints and advice. Some of these forums have archives where members post transcriptions of personal research data, family trees, photographs, and other useful information. Yahoo! Groups is host to many of these forums and, in my case, the Sociedad de Ancestros Mocanos (SAM) has been very productive, at https:// groups.yahoo.com/neo/groups/SAMocanos/info. SAM was founded in 2004, and one of its founding members and moderators served as the president of the California Genealogical Society. Like SAM, the other active Yahoo! Group is the Sociedad Puertorriqueña de Genealogía (SPG) at http://www.genealogiapr .com, an offshoot of the original.

Established in 1989, the SPG is the oldest and most important association for the scientific study of genealogy in Puerto Rico. Their official journal, *Hereditas*, publishes peer-reviewed works of genealogy and family history, to which many academics and professional genealogists contribute articles.

In addition to the SPG, Familysearch.org has opened several of their "Family History Centers," which act as intermediaries between localities and the microfilm, books, and other records and resources found in the centers' headquarters in Salt Lake City, Utah. As of 2014, there are eight of these centers in Puerto Rico: San Juan, Ponce, Mayagüez, Caguas, Arecibo, Toa Baja, Guayama, and Fajardo. Yet, most of the information that might be found at these centers may be found on their websites. The advantage of going in person to the centers is that someone can explain aspects of the database that are unclear online, or offer advice on research strategies.

Other online resources for recent genealogy with excellent information, articles, and even data sets, include Puerto Rico en Breve (http://www.preb .com/ref/geneal.htm) and the Puerto Rican/Hispanic Genealogical Society, Inc. (http://www.rootsweb.ancestry.com/~prhgs/).

Finally, oral history can serve as a quick and easy resource. Family members often have gathered information passed down from generation to generation. While some of that might be inaccurate, romanticized, or embellished, there is often a degree of truth in it, at least some hints to continue the document search. It is a matter of thinking critically about the information passed down by our older family members.

In regards to deep genealogy, some sources repeat the section above while some alternatives open new possibilities. Researchers should start by reading the article by Blanca Silvestrini-Pacheco and María de los Angeles Castro Arroyo (1981) on sources for Puerto Rican history. Additionally, researchers should consult the holdings at the Centro de Investigaciones Históricas of the University of Puerto Rico at Río Piedras. This center, created in 1946, holds a significant number of print and microfilmed materials from the sixteenth to the twentieth centuries. These were obtained locally and from archives in Spain, the US, and other Caribbean countries. A finding aid from 2013 can be accessed at http://archiredpr.files.wordpress.com/2010/06/guia-descriptiva3 .pdf. The new collection of sixteenth-century documents about Puerto Rico by Ricardo Alegría (2009), complements older collections, such as the *Actas del cabildo de San Juan Bautista de Puerto Rico* (1966; Hostos 1990–1995; Murga Sanz and Huerga 1961; Tapia y Rivera 1970; Tió 1961). Once again, genealogical forums and societies such as SAM and SPG are helpful. Except for some records from the San Juan Diocese (Castro and Castro 1991), due to the barely existent parish records from the 1500s and 1600s researching on the island is all but impossible.

Much research is yet to be done in Spanish archives, such as the Archivo General de Indias (AGI), Archivo Militar de Segovia, and the Archivo General de Simancas. Some records have been uploaded and many more indexed on the AGI's PARES Portal de Archivos Españoles site at http://pares.mcu.es/. Although PARES is a good way to start, they have not indexed many records, and a number of boxes in Puerto Rico are not accessible through the portal but in the archive waiting to be indexed. Similarly, records about Puerto Rico might be found in Mexico City, the site of the viceroyalty of New Spain. Due to the brief but significant occupation of Puerto Rico by the Dutch in 1625, there is a need to research Dutch archives. Researchers must also be familiar with and consult the different sections of the *Catálogo de pasajeros a Indias*, which covers all of Spanish America from the 1490s to the 1700s (Benzo de

Ferrer 2000; Bermúdez Plata 1940–46; Romera Iruela and Galbis Díez 1980; Rubio y Moreno 1927–32).

For deep genealogy, researchers must understand Puerto Rican, Caribbean, and Spanish history, both in and between the Peninsula and the New World. More than looking for names to fill up boxes in a family tree, the search for our ancestors can be a true learning experience. The researcher will be lost in the archive if there is no understanding of the historical context in which our ancestors lived. For example, in order to trace lineages into the seventeenth and sixteenth centuries it is crucial to understand that Puerto Rico was a peripheral area of the Spanish Empire that received few immigrants (Gelpí Baiz 2007; López Cantos 1975; Sued Badillo 2001; Vila Vilar 1974). Although there was constant migration from the Peninsula and neighboring islands to Puerto Rico between 1510 and 1550 (Sued Badillo 2001, 44–54), after the 1550s the Caribbean's relationship to the European continent became peripheral and increasing attention was paid to Peru and New Spain.

One must also understand the practice of intermarriage and social codes of honor and respectability that often dictated who was a good spousal candidate (López Cantos 2001). Oral history is also relevant in deep ancestry and is considered an essential tool for the history of Puerto Rico during the sixteenth and seventeenth centuries. Don Diego de Torres y Vargas's 1647 book, entitled *Descripción de la isla y ciudad de Puerto Rico, y de sus poblaciones, presidio, gobernadores y obispos; frutos y minerales*, was partly based on recollections of data through oral history (Stevens-Arroyo 2010).

Finally, another alternative for deep genealogy is DNA testing, a field in a constant state of flux and innovation. It is rather challenging to get started in this investigation as new discoveries and research findings arise almost monthly. However, the fundamentals of the field are simple and there is much reliable information on the web. There are a few basic ways to use DNA for genealogy. People can test their paternal lines directly into the past through a yDNA test, or their maternal lines through an mtDNA test. These can be as precise as to find relatives a few generations ago, such as second or third cousins, or the general areas where your ancestors lived ten thousand years ago. The third option is to test all lines from both sides through an autosomal DNA test.

To consider DNA testing, *Wikipedia* is a good starting point. As users get deeper into the subject, it is recommended they use up-to-date online forums because this is where they can learn about the most current information and recent discoveries. Forums range from specific closed groups on Facebook and Yahoo! Groups, to Anthrogenica.com. It is also good to consult the wiki page for the International Society for Genetic Genealogy (ISOGG). (http://www.isogg.org/wiki/Wiki_Welcome_Page). For users interested in trying out genetic genealogy, the leading company is Family Tree DNA. Founded in 2000, it is the oldest and most respected company in the field. Much of its clientele is North American or European, but a growing number of Iberian, African, Middle Eastern, and Asian descendants use it, as well. Other company sites are 23andme.com, AncestryDNA.com, and the National Geographic's Genographic Project, at https://genographic.nationalgeographic.com/. They have different missions and specialties, for some are better at recent genetic genealogy and others look into deep ancestry that dates to tens of thousands of years ago. Some are solely for genetic genealogy, while others include medical genetics in their results. Some people end up taking multiple tests with multiple companies to have a comprehensive understanding of their genetic makeup, but this can become expensive. The ISOGG has a useful table with each company's focus, missions, prices, and reviews, at: http://www.isogg.org/wiki/Autosomal_DNA_testing_comparison_chart.

Conclusion

Puerto Rican genealogy is not that different from that of other parts of the Caribbean. Places like the Dominican Republic, Cuba, Jamaica, Trinidad and Tobago, and Haiti lack resources due to climate and human-made damage. Places inhabited by Europeans some four hundred or five hundred years ago, but which only have documents back to some two hundred, greatly hinder genealogists. An even bigger factor, the introduction of African slaves who often did not have their ancestry recorded, makes black Caribbean genealogy even harder. In this case, oral history is an eminent resource, as well as DNA testing. Moreover, the latter reveals the strong presence of indigenous mitochondrial or mtDNA, and makes us seriously rethink the history of indigenous extinction (Via, et al. 2011).

Puerto Rican genealogy is experiencing a recent boom as has genealogy in other parts of the world. Websites, online databases, genealogy virtual groups and forums, have opened new lines of communication and information exchange that facilitates the study of our ancestors. Long-held ideas regarding genealogy as an activity of the upper classes, to find or corroborate important ancestors, are slowly fading, yet have not totally disappeared. However, while still hoping to find that extraordinary ancestor, people are also trying to discover, confirm, or explore family legends and lore passed down through generations, or are simply curious about their family history. As librarians we must understand the rapidly changing field of genealogy, and be able to discern good resources from unreliable ones.

This article has introduced the common problems in Caribbean genealogy and reliable alternatives to engage in this fascinating field. Genealogy is mainly done by untrained researchers, thus there is fertile ground to produce or reproduce inaccurate and often outright false information. Stories of great, even mythological, ancestors abound and need to be confronted with historical rigor. For example, the Sotomayors are said to have descended from Hercules! Researchers are encouraged to do genealogy after having read reliable historical secondary sources to understand the context in which their ancestors might have lived. Indeed, a genealogical researcher should confirm the existence of an individual by using two reliable primary sources. Among those are censuses, vital records, wills and testaments, and notarial records. With the rapid increase in DNA testing, users need all the more to understand the science behind a fast-growing field. In this regard, online genetic genealogy sites such as Anthrogenica.com and the ISOGG wiki are recommended due to their reliability.

Overall, it seems that genealogy is not going away, as long as the tradition of inheriting last names persists. Because of this, it is important for librarians, both public and academic, to pay more attention to this field, in order to teach users to find, evaluate, and interpret information.

REFERENCES

Acosta, Ursula, and David E. Cuesta Camacho. 1983. *Familias de Cabo Rojo.* Hormigueros, PR.

Actas del cabildo de San Juan Bautista de Puerto Rico. 1966. San Juan, PR: Publicación Oficial del Gobierno de la Capital.

Alegría, Ricardo. 2009. *Documentos históricos de Puerto Rico.* San Juan, PR: Centro de Estudios Avanzados de Puerto Rico y El Caribe.

Armstrong Mejía de Blila, Elba, and Luis A. Villares Armstrong. 2000. *Familia: La historia de los Armstrong en Puerto Rico.* Caguas, PR: Publicaciones LV.

Barragán Landa, Juan José. 1996. *Los Benítez: Raices de una familia hacedora de historia.* Puerto Rico.

Benzo de Ferrer, Vilma. 2000. *Pasajeros a la Española, 1492–1530.* Santo Domingo, República Dominicana.

Bermúdez Plata, Cristóbal. 1940–46. *Catálogo de pasajeros a Indias durante los siglos XVI, XVII y XVIII.* Volúmenes I, II, III (1509–1559). Sevilla: Imprenta Editorial de la Gavidia.

Borges, Dain. 1992. *The Family in Bahia, Brazil, 1870–1945.* Stanford: Stanford University Press.

Casanova Laforet, Gustavo. 1982. *Esbozos genealógicos: Familias Cabo Rojo y Mayagüez, Puerto Rico; Apuntes biográficos e históricos.* Carolina, PR.

Castro, Teresa de, and Lorraine de Castro. 1991. *Rescate del libro primero de matrimonios de la santa yglesia catedral de San Juan de Puerto Rico Nuestra Señora de los Remedios.* Puerto Rico.

Colón Gaulden, Edmund. 1988. *Colón Families of the Seventeenth Century in Puerto Rico: Their Roots and Notable Descendants.* Orange, CA.

Cuesta Camacho, David, and Adolfo Pérez Comas. n.d. *Juan Ponce de León, el Adelantado: Su entorno familiar y algunas proyecciones familiares en Puerto Rico.* Puerto Rico.

Dávila Valldejuli, José. 1995. *Genealogía Valldejuli, Duprey y Roqué de Puerto Rico.* Lubbock, TX: printed by author.

Delgado Plasencia, Enrique. 1998. *Parientes isleños, hatillanos, lejanos y cercanos: García-Díaz, García-Delgado, Plasencia-García, Casanova-García.* n.p., Puerto Rico: printed by author.

———. 2009. *Ramas y raíces de los Delgado y Abreu: Los descendientes de Fernándo Delgado de Abreu y Juliana Delgado Garabato.* San Juan, PR.

El-Haj, Nadia Abu. 2007. "Rethinking Genetic Genealogy: A Response to Stephan Palmié." *American Ethnologist* 34 (2): 223–26.

Encarnación Navarro, Carlos. 2005. *Genealogías y crónicas del siglo 19: Tomo segundo.* San Juan, PR: Impresora Oriental, Inc.

Fitzpatrick, Colleen, and Andrew Yeiser. 2005. *DNA and Genealogy.* Fountain Valley, CA: Rice Book Press.

Font, Cecilio R. 1987. *Primera aproximación a las familias Font, Etxeandía.* El Pepino, PR.

García de la Concha, Víctor. 2014. *La Real Academia Española. Vida e historia.* Barcelona: Espasa Calpe.

Gaudier, Martín. 1963–64. *Genealogias puertorriqueñas; partidas de bautismos y biografías.* Puerto Rico.

Gelpí Baiz, Elsa. 2007. *Siglo en blanco: Estudio de la economía azucarera en Puerto Rico del siglo XVI (1540–1612).* San Juan: Editorial de la Universidad de Puerto Rico.

Gil-Loyzaga, Pablo E. 2007. *Cuatro siglos en Puerto Rico: descendientes de Antonio de los Reyes Correa y de Diego R. Colón de Luyando y sus vínculos familiares con los Loyzaga, Mexía-Casado y Rodríguez de Matos en los siglos XVI al XIX.* Madrid: Vision Net.

Hostos, Adolfo de. 1990–95. *Tesauro de datos históricos de Puerto Rico: Índice compendioso de la literatura histórica de Puerto Rico, incluyendo algunos datos inéditos, periodísticos y cartográficos.* Río Piedras: Editorial de la Universidad de Puerto Rico.

Huerga, Álvaro. 2008. *La familia Torres y Vargas Zapata.* San Juan: Academia Puertorriqueña de la Historia: Centro de Estudios Avanzados de Puerto Rico y del Caribe: Fundación Puertorriqueña de las Humanidades.

———. 2009. *La familia Ponce de León.* San Juan: Academia Puertorriqueña de la Historia: Centro de Estudios Avanzados de Puerto Rico y del Caribe: Fundación Puertorriqueña de las Humanidades.

Pomery, Chris. 2007. *Family History in the Genes: Trace Your DNA and Grow Your Family Tree.* Kew, UK: National Archives.

Larmuseau, M.H.D., A. Van Geystelen, M. Van Oven, and R. Decorte. 2013. "Genetic Genealogy Comes of Age: Perspectives on the Use of Deep-Rooted Pedigrees in Human Population Genetics." *American Journal of Physical Anthropology* 150 (4): 505–11.

Lluch Mora, Francisco. 1976. *Catálogo de inscripciones demográfico-sacramentales y de otra índole del linaje puertorriqueño Ortiz de la Renta.* Puerto Rico: Fundación Juan C. Ortiz de la Renta Lugo.

Lockhart, James. 1994. *Spanish Perú, 1532–1560*. Madison: The University of Wisconsin Press.

López Cantos, Ángel. 1975. *Historia de Puerto Rico, 1650–1700*. Sevilla, España: Escuela de Estudios Hispano-Americanos.

———. 2000. *Los puertorriqueños: mentalidad y actitudes, siglo XVIII*. San Juan: Editorial de la Universidad de Puerto Rico.

Machado Martínez, Eduardo. 1999. *Historia de Juan Machado Díaz y sus descendientes*. Puerto Rico: printed by author.

Martínez Nazario, Manuel. 2004a. *Estudio genealógico de la ascendencia materna de Isabel Suárez y de Castro*. San Juan, PR.

———. 2004b. *Genealogía de las familias Martínez, Detrés, Nazario, Oliveras y López*. San Juan, PR.

Mayoral Barnés, Manuel. 1946. *Ponce y su historial geopolítico-económico y cultural: Con el árbol genealógico de sus pobladores*. Ponce, PR.

Murga Sanz, Vicente, and Álvaro Huerga. 1961. *Cedulario puertorriqueño. Tomo I (1505–1517)*. Río Piedras: Editorial de la Universidad de Puerto Rico.

Negroni, Héctor Andrés. 1998. *The Negroni Family: Genealogical, Demographic, and Nobiliary Study from its 11th Century Origins to its 20th Century Branches in Italy, France, and Puerto Rico*. Madison, AL: H. A. Negroni.

Nieves Acevedo, Benjamín. 2009. *Historia de Aguada: Siglos XVI–XIX*. Aguada, PR: Editorial Aymaco.

Nieves Méndez, Antonio. 2004. *Historia de un pueblo: Moca 1772 al 2000*. Aguada, PR: Editorial Aymaco.

Oquendo Pabón, José Antonio. 2000. *Familias de mi terruño: Árboles genealógicos*. St. Petersburg, FL: Raíces de Muertito Heaven, Inc.

Platt, Lyman De. 1990. *Puerto Rico: Research Guide*. Salt Lake City: Instituto Genealógico e Histórico Latinoamericano.

Ramírez Brau, Enrique. 1947. *Orígenes puertorriqueños (Don Antonio Ramírez de Arellano y sus descendientes) … del año 1653 al 1853*. San Juan, PR: Imprenta Baldrich.

Reed, Robert D., and Danek S. Kaus. 1994. *How and Where to Research Your Ethnic-American Cultural Heritage: Puerto Rican Americans*. San Jose, CA: R & E Publishers.

Rodríguez León, Mario A. 1983. "Los registros parroquiales y la microhistoria demográfica en Puerto Rico." Masters thesis, Centro de Estudios Avanzados de Puerto Rico y el Caribe.

Romera Iruela, Luis, and María del Carmen Galbis Díez. 1980. *Catálogo de pasajeros a Indias durante los siglos XVI, XVII y XVIII*. Volúmenes IV y V (1560–1577). Madrid: Ministerio de Cultura.

Rosado, Samuel. 1994. *As for My Ancestors: A Brief in Detail History of the Rosado Family from Puerto Rico*. New York, NY: S. Rosado.

Rubio y Moreno, Luis. 1927–32. *Pasajeros a Indias: Colección de documentos inéditos para la historia de Hispano-América*. Tomos II y III (1492–1592). Madrid: Compañía Ibero-Americana de Publicaciones.

Ryskamp, George R. 2000. "The Intergenerational Transmission of Surnames in Spain, 1500–1900." In *La Vie Genealogique* 28 *(Acts of the 24th International Congress on Genealogical and Heraldic Sciences, Besançon, France, May 5–7):* 317–30.

———. June 2002. "The De Lema Dilemma: Exploring the Complexities of Spanish Naming Patterns." *National Genealogical Society Quarterly* 90: 87–98.

———. June 2003. "Genealogical Research in the Basque Country." *Genealogical Journal, An International Publication*, 31: 76–87.

———. 2005. "La transmisión de apellidos en España y las Colonias americanas (1500–1900)." In *Actas de la XI Reunión Americana de Genealogía. España y América, un escenario común*, edited by Eduardo Pardo de Guevara y Valdés, 341–64. Santiago de Compostela.

Sáez, Florencio. 1995. *Guayanilla, Barrio Pasto: Genealogía del apellido Sáez*. Puerto Rico: Editorial Palma Real.

Santiago Torres, José. 1986. *Nuestros ancestros: Estudio genealógico: historia de los apellidos Sellés-Aponte de San Lorenzo, Solá-López de Caguas*. n.p.

Schmal, John P. 1994. *A Puerto Rican Family: The Peña-Carrasquillo Family History*. California: J.P. Schmal.

Silvestrini-Pacheco, Blanca, and María de los Angeles Castro Arroyo. 1981. "Sources for the Study of Puerto Rican History." *Latin American Research Review* 16 (2): 156–71.

Solivan de Acosta, Jaime A. 1988. *Cinco familias linajudas en Puerto Rico*. Puerto Rico.

———. 1993. *El general oscense don Felipe Perena y su descendencia en Puerto Rico*. Puerto Rico.

———. 1996. *Don Pedro Velarde y su descendencia Aragonés-Puertorriqueña*. Carolina, PR: First Book Publishers of P.R.

Stark, David. 2002. "The Family Tree Is Not Cut: Marriage among Slaves in Eighteenth-Century Puerto Rico." *New West Indian Guide* 76 (1&2): 23–45.

———. 2006. "Parish Registers as a Window to the Past: Reconstructing the Demographic Behavior of the Enslaved Population in Eighteenth-Century Arecibo, Puerto Rico." *Colonial Latin American Historical Review* 15 (1): 1–30.

Stevens-Arroyo, Anthony M. 2010. "Understanding the Work of Diego de Torres y Vargas." In Torres y Vargas 2010, 8–9.

Sued Badillo, Jalil. 2001. *El Dorado Borincano: La economía de la Conquista: 1510–1550*. San Juan, PR: Ediciones Puerto.

Tapia y Rivera, Alejandro. 1970. *Obras completas Tapia y Rivera 3 Biblioteca histórica de Puerto-Rico, que contiene varios documentos de los siglos XV, XVI, XVII y XVIII*. San Juan, Puerto Rico: Instituto de Literatura Puertorriqueña.

Tió, Aurelio. 1961. *Nuevas fuentes para la historia de Puerto Rico: Documentos inéditos o poco conocidos cuyos originales se encuentran en el Archivo General de Indias en la ciudad de Sevilla, España*. San Germán: Ediciones de la Universidad Interamericana de Puerto Rico.

Torres y Vargas, Don Diego. 2010. *Report on the Island and Diocese of Puerto Rico (1647).* Translated by Jaime R. Vidal. Scranton: University of Scranton Press.

Via, Marc. et al. 2001. "History Shaped the Geographic Distribution of Genomic Admixture on the Island of Puerto Rico." *PLoS ONE* 6 (1): e16513. doi:10.1371/journal.pone.0016513.

Vila, Suso. 2010. *A casa de Soutomaior (1147–1532).* Noia, A Coruña, Galicia: Editorial Toxosoutos.

Vila Vilar, Enriqueta. 1974. *Historia de Puerto Rico, 1600–1650.* Sevilla, España: Escuela de Estudios Hispano-Americanos.

9. Shaping Student Learning through Embedded Librarianship in Area Studies

Betsaida M. Reyes

The majority of articles published on embedded librarianship focus on its benefits or discuss how embedded librarians integrate themselves in courses. Few articles describe the long-term effects of embedded librarianship in a traditional course for graduate students, particularly in area studies. Embedded librarianship can be applied to a variety of circumstances and thus, for the purposes of this paper, the term is used to describe the role of the librarian in which their duties "generally involve activities outside of the library" (Rudasill 2010, 84). Embedded also describes "any librarian that takes an active role inside the online classroom" (Becker 2010, 237). Whether the class is online or in a traditional face-to-face setting, the level of involvement is fairly similar.

Background

Prior to the fall of 2013, the Center for Latin American & Caribbean Studies (CLACS) at the University of Kansas (KU) had a research class, "LAA 700: Latin American Library Resources." This class was taught by the subject librarian. However, preceding my arrival at the University of Kansas, it was decided that it would be taught by faculty in the Global and International Studies Graduate Program (GIS Graduate) and cross-listed in the CLACS Department. I reached out to GIS faculty to discuss possible options to continue to be involved in the class even though it was now part of another program's curriculum. My goal was to be part of the class rather than to provide just one information literacy session during the semester. Over the summer months, the two assigned faculty members and I maintained close contact to ensure good integration of information literacy skills in the class. They were in charge of the development of the syllabus while I ran the information literacy portion of the class. The class program specified that I would be a guest lecturer once during the semester. In practice, I attended over 40 percent of the class meetings.

The class included twelve students, four from Latin American and Caribbean Studies and eight from the Global and International Graduate

Who Are We Really?: Latin American Family, Local and Micro-Regional Histories, and Their Impact on Understanding Ourselves. Papers of the Fifty-Ninth Annual Meeting of SALALM, 2014.

Studies Program. As a co-teacher for this class, I had permission to access the learning management system, Blackboard, as a "Teacher Assistant." This allowed me to view students' responses to assignments as well as to post notes and PowerPoint presentations from class.

I was present during the first class of the semester, and was introduced to the students as the librarian who was going to be in most of the classes. I chose to sit amongst the students, in an effort to become part of their group rather than as an instructor figure. I took notes of which semester the students were in, their research interests, and projects. My primary role in the class was to offer research support and not to grade them.

Five classes into the semester it was my turn to stand in front of the class. This group's level of research skills was not apparent, so the first part of the lesson was a quick review of the resources available to them at the University of Kansas Libraries. This review included items like "turning a question into search terms," searching the catalog and selected databases, and using inter-library loan. The second part of the lesson was focused entirely on individual research questions. The topics covered a wide area of disciplines as well as geographical locations. Examples included: the increase in sex trafficking in connection with large sporting events, the feasibility of hemp as a sustainable crop for Paraguay, and the viability of importing water from Russia to help alleviate its scarcity in China.

There was no overlap between research questions or approaches to locating information, and this made the second part of the class less organized. I had to go to each student to lead them in the right direction with their research question. This task took more time than scheduled. At the students' request, and after some revision and added information, the class presentation was uploaded to Blackboard.

Communication between the teaching faculty and the librarian are key components to the success of the collaboration. It allows the librarian to tailor subsequent lessons to correspond with students' development (Miller 2014, 31). For the second lesson in research, I teamed up with the faculty to create an assignment that tied the previous information literacy session in with the rest of the class program. Students had to answer two questions:

1. Which of the resources discussed in class or available through the library will be the most useful for your thesis research? Why?

2. Keeping your research project in mind, give specific examples (two or three) of primary or secondary sources found in any of the databases discussed in class. (Please indicate whether it is a primary or secondary source and, in a couple of sentences, discuss how you will be able to utilize this source in your work.)

Patterns began to emerge from the responses to the assignment. Among the most listed resources were the KU catalog, WorldCat, *Bibliography of Asian*

Studies, Google Scholar, *EconLit*, and the World Bank Database. Some students noted services like interlibrary loan and LibGuides. Several also mentioned the usefulness of tools within the databases. These included the "cited by" option in Google Scholar, and the option to narrow one's results in Business Source Complete. Students continuously referred to a book or an article as their primary resource for their individual projects. Having access to Blackboard proved invaluable on this occasion. It was apparent that students referred to the main source for their research as their primary one. To bridge this gap, I created a handout explaining the differences between primary and secondary sources. This handout was shared in the second class. Students discussed their own knowledge of primary and secondary sources in contrast to the definitions provided on the handout.

I taught two more sessions covering statistical sources and archival documents, and also continued to provide one-on-one consultations for the students throughout the rest of the class. Many of the students maintained communication with me in the spring semester via email or face-to-face consultations. The majority came in for research assistance, while others emailed regarding questions with interlibrary loan or purchase requests. Throughout these consultation sessions, students volunteered information regarding the class, which caused me to reevaluate and draw new boundaries.

Measuring Student Learning Impact

Throughout the semester, I met with the assigned faculty members regularly and discussed the importance of measuring how student learning had been affected after taking the class. A small focus group was chosen as the ideal way to gather feedback. It was determined that the focus group would be held after the semester, to avoid lack of participation or cooperation due to impending grades. It was also decided that the faculty would not be present during the focus group to allow students the opportunity to provide honest and unbiased feedback.

A Doodle Poll was created to determine students' time availability. The response rate was 33 percent or only four students. The low participation rate had a variety of causes, including but not limited to students dropping out of the program, or living outside Lawrence where the main campus is located.

I met the four students for one hour, during which nine questions were discussed. The questions were divided between general ones about the class experience and those related to a librarian's participation in the class. Since distance was one of the reasons why some students did not participate in the focus group, a short survey was created using Google Forms and was distributed among those who did not respond to the meeting call. This approach returned two more responses, which increased the response rate to 50 percent or a total of six participants. The summary and discussion of responses that follows is a mixture of the information gathered in the focus group, as well as data from the survey responses.

When asked about their overall experience in taking the course, the comments of students generally fell into one of two categories. On one hand, it was an enjoyable experience since it exposed them to various methods of research. On the other, they felt that the course load was on the heavy side.

One student complained that the class was so time-consuming that it did not leave room to work on developing his own research project, the very one he needed to graduate. Another student felt that by covering so many methods the students were not studying any of them in depth. As a follow-up, a second student remarked that, "it was much harder to complete assignments when the method does not apply to your research project."

Given that the course was co-taught by two faculty members and I was only there in a supportive role, students were questioned if it was helpful to have two instructors. It was a surprise to hear the majority of students remark on how useful it was to have a librarian in the class, but the role of the second teacher was almost entirely overlooked since his presence was so infrequent. Students agreed that he came in only once to lecture and, in their minds, this did not make him a class co-instructor. Instead, they felt that I filled that role.

Along those lines, students also remarked that the expertise of their primary teacher in research methodology, in conjunction with that of a librarian in class, was very helpful. The inclusion of a librarian had a causal effect in their overall perception of the library. For some of them it was a chance to realize that libraries offer many more services beyond lending books. For others it opened the door to establish a relationship that will continue well into the end of their program. Students were made aware at the beginning of the class that they were welcome to come in and seek my assistance for their projects. My schedule was far more open and flexible than the restrictive office hours of faculty. This contrast allowed students more opportunities to develop a relationship with their librarian, and to really spend time working on their research topics with the help of someone who was familiar with their class. It also created some unexpected situations. On one occasion, a student asked me to proofread a paper (the paper was for a spring semester symposium). While the door was always open for almost anything before, it became apparent that "an embedded librarian should set boundaries" (Becker 2010, 239).

Students were asked what elements of the class they had found most helpful. The answers discussed centered on concerns or suggestions for future classes, rather than the elements that did work for them. A few insightful remarks, however, showed that they did find some things beneficial. One of the students commented that the class structure, with various deadlines for the assignments, helped get the thesis and literature review underway.

There were many suggestions offered to improve the course, ranging from when and where to offer it, to how many days a week it should be taught. The class was offered through the Global and International Program, based in our Kansas City location, Edwards Campus. The majority of the students enrolled in it were based in Lawrence so, to attend the evening class, they had to travel thirty-three miles in each direction once a week. Not all of the students had a car to make the trip, so they either relied on other students to get a ride or took the bus. The last option invariably made their trip twice as long. Some students also thought it would be good to have the class twice a week rather than just once. This would allow them more time to better digest the material.

Though gathering information on students' experiences in this class was highly important for its future, my primary interest lay in an embedded librarian's impact on the students' research process in the long run. No data regarding students' research ability or confidence was gathered prior to their taking the class. The data collected in the focus group and through the online survey was all based on students' perception of changes in their own abilities over time.

Students were asked about their confidence level in doing research before and after the class. Some respondents identified themselves as "not very comfortable" when doing research prior to the class. Some of the reasons why they did not feel confident had to do with their lack of knowledge about services, tools, and databases; for example, services like interlibrary loan, the use of subject or LibGuides, and the legitimacy of Google Scholar. Since Google's search engine is a commercial platform, students did not know that they could find reliable resources there. Students also discovered that using Google Scholar in tandem with the library's databases could be highly effective and efficient. Many students reported not having been aware of LibGuides. However, when they began to take classes in other departments due to the interdisciplinarity of their degree program, they continued to use LibGuides after the research methods class was over. Other students commented on how their exposure to new databases broadened their options when doing research. As a result of including a librarian in the class, many students became knowledgeable of the various services the libraries had to offer. One service that students discovered during this methods class was interlibrary loan. Through later interactions with students as they worked to complete their Master's theses, it became apparent how interlibrary loan empowered them to successfully complete their exhaustive research.

Though there was an improvement in their research abilities and confidence after taking the class, it is important to highlight that this was not the case for all students. Some felt that they were doing a good job at locating the sources they needed for their projects prior to the class, thus reporting that there was not much more to be learned in the course. Most students felt more confident doing research but those who did not at least learned where they could get the help they needed.

Conclusion

Embedded librarianship is much more than the latest buzzword in the library community. The benefit and long-lasting effects are tangible and measurable. The presence of a librarian in a classroom can help create a relationship with the students similar to the ones they have with their professors. The benefits of such a relationship become clearer when we see that students are more likely to ask an instructor than a librarian for help finding books or journal articles (Mazurkiewicz and Potts 2007, 168). The overlap in instructor and librarian roles makes it possible for some students to continue visiting the librarian for help with their research, even after the class is over. The students come to value the librarian as a resource and continue to seek his or her assistance throughout their program. In general "students are more willing to seek help when they know a librarian is an integral part of the class" (Becker 2010, 238). This is evidence that librarians need to continue to reach out to the students and faculty beyond our offices. However, it is also important to keep scalability in mind. The time commitment of an embedded librarian is far greater than what's needed for a one-shot session of instruction. Librarians are assigned to multiple subjects with dozens of faculty and hundreds of students to work with. This means that it is simply impossible to provide the same level of service to all of them. A class on research methods or a thesis seminar is an ideal option to maximize our impact on student learning.

Suggestions for Future Embedded Librarians

The following suggestions are based on my experiences:

1. Be proactive. Propose a collaboration of embedded librarianship to a receptive faculty member. Though the faculty makes many of the decisions regarding how and when librarians teach information literacy, you can still suggest how you can be most useful to them.

2. Familiarize yourself with students' class research interests/projects. Rather than starting from scratch, this will save you time when you provide guidance on locating their topical information. Take notes from the classes you attend.

3. Do not be afraid to ask the teaching faculty for more class time. Though being an embedded librarian signifies being more involved in the class, it does not mean that you have to fit a complex lesson into one session because the syllabus says that you are only teaching one day. Talk to the faculty with whom you collaborate, and estimate how much time is needed to cover the necessary material. After all, they want you in their classroom.

4. Ask students and faculty for feedback on how to improve the class. This will improve your relationship with them and, in turn, your teaching strategies.

5. Be flexible with your time. Despite the fact that you are not grading them, students will view you as an authority figure and thus seek your advice during the semester. For example, they will come for help at the last minute, or ask questions after class.

REFERENCES

Becker, Bernd W. 2010. "Embedded Librarianship: A Point-of-Need Service." *Behavioral & Social Sciences Librarian* 29, no. 3: 237–40. doi:10.1080/01639269. 2010.498763

Mazurkiewicz, Orchid, and Claude H. Potts. 2007. "Researching Latin America: A Survey of How the New Generation Is Doing its Research." *Latin American Research Review* 42, no. 3: 161–82.

Miller, Robin E. 2014. "Sauté, Simmer, Reduce: Embedded Lessons in the Research Process for First-Year Composition Students." In *The Embedded Librarian's Cookbook*, edited by Kaijsa Calkins and Cassandra Kvenild, 28–31. Chicago: Association of College and Research Libraries.

Rudasill, Lynne Marie. 2010. "Beyond Subject Specialization: The Creation of Embedded Librarians." *Public Services Quarterly* 6, no. 2–3: 83–91. doi:10.1080 /15228959.2010.494577

10. Revistas culturales de América Latina: Un proyecto de adquisición y digitalización del Instituto Ibero-Americano, Berlín

Ricarda Musser

Situación inicial

Una prioridad en las tareas de adquisición y catalogación del Instituto Ibero-Americano (IAI) es digitalizar las colecciones de cultura popular latinoamericana, cuyos orígenes se remontan a la Biblioteca Criolla del antropólogo alemán Robert Lehmann-Nitsche, adquirida ya en el año 1939. Con las adiciones realizadas hasta la fecha, la colección de Lehmann-Nitsche comprende unos 2100 cuadernos de literatura popular argentina. Durante los últimos diez a quince años, se siguieron adquiriendo, con medios propios, amplios fondos de literatura popular de distintos países, por ejemplo, la colección de revistas teatrales y novelas cortas argentinas, que ya abarca unos 6500 cuadernillos, y la de literatura de cordel brasileña, que proviene de la literatura popular del nordeste de Brasil, y está compuesta de más de 8000 *folhetos* hasta la fecha. También se han llevado a cabo, con fondos tanto propios como externos, extensas tareas de catalogación y clasificación, por ejemplo, del legado de Robert Lehmann-Nitsche, y de la colección mexicana de José Guadalupe Posada, que abarca más de 100 cuadernillos y unos 450 pliegos sueltos. Todas las colecciones mencionadas tienen un carácter único en Alemania. En su mayoría, datan de entre finales del siglo XIX y el primer tercio del siglo XX. En la medida de lo permitido por los derechos de autor, estas colecciones ya están disponibles en versión digital o están siendo objeto de proyectos de digitalización del Instituto Ibero-Americano.

La adquisición, catalogación y digitalización de revistas culturales se enmarca en el contexto de estas colecciones debido a que por su espectro temático y de presentación, estas publicaciones constituyen un vínculo ideal entre la alta cultura y la cultura popular.

Who Are We Really?: Latin American Family, Local and Micro-Regional Histories, and Their Impact on Understanding Ourselves. Papers of the Fifty-Ninth Annual Meeting of SALALM, 2014.

Clasificación científica de las revistas culturales

Es difícil formular una definición precisa de lo que son las revistas culturales. De hecho, las fuentes secundarias sobre este medio suelen advertir de que no es posible distinguir con precisión entre este formato de revista y otros similares. En cuanto a su contenido, las revistas culturales abordan los más diversos temas. Ello nos remite a un concepto muy amplio de cultura, que incluye no sólo las humanidades orientadas a los estudios culturales, sino también y, expresamente, las ciencias naturales. La interdisciplinariedad ha sido probablemente el principal rasgo distintivo de las revistas culturales publicadas entre 1880 y 1930. Los múltiples tópicos en ellas tratados incluían política, literatura, teoría musical, así como artículos prácticos, sociológicos, satíricos y técnicos. Los textos se redactaban con la intención de que fuesen comprensibles para un público general, de forma que atrajesen a lectores tanto académicos como no académicos, y el formato de los artículos era tan variado como sus contenidos. Fuentes primarias y secundarias compartían un espacio con entrevistas, reseñas, críticas, noticias y caricaturas. La mayoría de las revistas culturales también contenían numerosos gráficos, ilustraciones y fotografías. Además, eran un medio apreciado para fines publicitarios, al igual que para anuncios de contactos y breves.

Por su riqueza de imágenes, las revistas culturales también reflejaban, de forma muy ilustrativa, (en fotos, dibujos y gráficos), las condiciones sociales de los países de América Latina y el Caribe en el periodo seleccionado. Sus lectores eran muy heterogéneos. Así, las revistas culturales alcanzaban distintas capas sociales, pero también distintos sexos y edades. De hecho, su amplia recepción no puede medirse considerando exclusivamente la correspondiente tirada, ya que en el seno de las familias y en espacios públicos, como cafeterías y bibliotecas, las revistas pasaban por incontables manos.

Por todo lo anterior, cabe atribuir a las revistas culturales una alta relevancia social y cultural. Los intelectuales y los artistas las empleaban para expresarse, interviniendo así en la vida política y cultural. Los debates en ellas publicados podían dar lugar a discursos sociales en general y corrientes artísticas en particular. Fue así como las revistas culturales tuvieron una participación directa en la formación de cánones literarios. También jugaron un papel importante en la transmisión, configuración y continuación de tradiciones (locales, regionales y nacionales), y en el proceso de formación de naciones y de integración de grandes grupos heterogéneos de población dentro de la infraestructura sociocultural y político-jurídica de estados independientes a menudo todavía muy jóvenes. Les correspondió, en definitiva, un rol destacado en la construcción de la identidad nacional y cultural.

No obstante, las revistas culturales no solían restringirse a una visión puramente nacional. Las relaciones internacionales entre países vecinos y el proceso de integración regional en América Latina se veían reflejados en distintos artículos de las revistas culturales. ¿Cómo se reseñaban las obras literarias en los distintos países? ¿Qué obras se traducían, cuándo y dónde? ¿Qué papel desempeñaban las antiguas potencias coloniales u otros países europeos en la vida cultural y cómo eran representados? En este contexto, deben destacarse también las publicaciones de asociaciones culturales extranjeras, por ejemplo, las revistas franco-argentinas. Al respecto, cabe constatar un gran interés científico por realizar investigaciones sobre la migración y el exilio, y la historia de la inmigración en Latinoamérica.

Como fuentes científicas, las revistas culturales latinoamericanas de finales del siglo XIX y principios del siglo XX tienen una gran relevancia en múltiples aspectos. De la interdisciplinariedad de sus contenidos, resultan intereses de investigación también interdisciplinarios, tales como la literatura, los estudios culturales, la historia, la sociología y la lingüística. Las revistas culturales para mujeres o las páginas dedicadas especialmente a mujeres dentro de las revistas culturales abren otro campo de investigación dentro de los estudios de género. Hasta ahora, su investigación sistemática en Alemania ha sido posible solo en parte porque estas fuentes no estaban disponibles de forma suficientemente completa en ninguna biblioteca. No obstante, el elevado número de solicitudes de beca que llegan al IAI, con el firme propósito de investigar materiales de cultura popular o materiales que vinculan la alta cultura con la cultura popular, sugiere que el interés de los investigadores aún sigue siendo muy grande.

Parámetros del proyecto y fases de trabajo

Desde mediados del año 2013, la Biblioteca del Instituto Ibero-Americano viene desarrollando un proyecto para la adquisición, catalogación, clasificación y digitalización de revistas culturales latinoamericanas, con el apoyo financiero de la Deutsche Forschungsgemeinschaft (DFG, Fundación Alemana para la Investigación Científica, www.dfg.de), en el programa Föderung herausragender Forschungsbibliotheken (Bibliotecas de Excelencia en la Investigación). El proyecto tiene una duración de treinta y seis meses. Para la adquisición de revistas culturales destinadas a este proyecto, se seleccionaron países de los cuales el Instituto Ibero-Americano posee ya algunos títulos, usualmente en colecciones incompletas, o países en los que, según los resultados del estudio de mercado, existen posibilidades reales de compra, ya sea en formato digital, microfilm o papel. Los países seleccionados —Argentina, Chile, Cuba, Ecuador, Perú y Puerto Rico— reflejan demandas concretas de la comunidad científica y conforman una muestra geográfica representativa de la colección del IAI. En la medida de lo permitido por los derechos del autor, las revistas se digitalizan en el IAI, siguiendo el *Goobi workflow*, y se ponen a disposición del público a través del catálogo en línea OPAC de la biblioteca del instituto (www.iaicat.de) y en la plataforma de las Colecciones Digitales del IAI (www.iaidigital.de). Goobi hace posibles proyectos de digitalización en bibliotecas, archivos y museos. El programa informático en que se basa es flexible y apto para las más variadas estrategias de digitalización. El flujo de trabajo se ha perfeccionado y se ha adaptado a las necesidades del IAI sobre la base de trabajos preparatorios de la Biblioteca Estatal y Universitaria de Gotinga, de la Biblioteca Estatal de Sajonia y Universitaria de Dresde, así como de la Biblioteca Estatal de Berlín, la cual, al igual que el IAI, pertenece a la Fundación Patrimonio Cultural Prusiano.

La distribución por países de los títulos seleccionados para el proyecto es la siguiente: Argentina: 31; Chile: 10; Cuba: 10; Ecuador: 10; Perú: 14; Puerto Rico: 6. (Todos los títulos se encuentran enumerados en el apéndice). En total, la colección se complementará retrospectivamente con alrededor de 17 415 fascículos, con un precio medio de 10 euros por ejemplar, según cálculos orientativos.

En la primera fase del trabajo de adquisición, se reunieron y aceptaron, en la medida de lo posible, ofertas de compra actuales de instituciones y librerías de viejo ya conocidas por el IAI, dando prioridad a las ofertas digitales. De no haberlas, se piden ofertas de microformas cuya conservación disminuirá considerablemente los costos, mucho más que las ediciones impresas.

Debido a que la experiencia de los últimos años ha demostrado que numerosas ofertas, en especial en lo que respecta a las colecciones especiales, solo pueden hacerse y cerrarse *in situ*, se realizarán dos viajes de adquisición con el propósito expreso de adquirir los números que faltan en la colección de revistas culturales. Las posibilidades de compra son muy diferentes en cada uno de los países seleccionados.

En Argentina, con sus numerosas librerías de viejo, al menos en la capital, Buenos Aires, es generalmente factible encontrar las revistas que faltan. Además, los viajes de adquisición realizados en los últimos años resultan en ofertas especiales para el Instituto Ibero-Americano, como ocurrió en el caso de la adquisición de la revista folclórico-literaria *Nativa*. El IAI, que poseía pocos ejemplares, tuvo la oportunidad de comprar, a la viuda del último editor, todos los números de la revista, incluyendo el último, aún inédito. Tras su digitalización, los ejemplares de *Nativa* están disponibles al público por primera vez en su totalidad.

En pasados viajes de adquisición a Perú, también se han tenido buenas experiencias en cuanto a la compra de revistas históricas, aunque el contacto con libreros especializados en materiales antiguos en este país no es tan estrecho como en Argentina.

En Chile, los originales que se buscan se encuentran en las librerías de viejo solo excepcionalmente. No obstante, el IAI tiene estrechos contactos con la Biblioteca Nacional de Chile y con Memoria Chilena, plataforma en la que ya están disponibles, en formato virtual, cuatro de las revistas culturales integradas en el proyecto (www.memoriachilena.cl). Para estos casos, en el catálogo del IAI, hay un enlace con las copias digitalizadas ya existentes. En el futuro, esperamos poder intercambiar también metadatos con la Biblioteca Nacional de Chile.

Las relaciones de trabajo con la Biblioteca Nacional de Cuba, también iniciadas hace muchos años, sirven para cooperar en la digitalización de las revistas culturales que forman parte del proyecto y para el intercambio de archivos digitalizados.

En Puerto Rico, es prácticamente imposible adquirir ejemplares originales, pero la Universidad de Puerto Rico se ha ofrecido elaborar una copia en microfilm de su colección de revistas culturales para el Instituto Ibero-Americano.

En las librerías de Quito, existen muchos títulos de revistas culturales de Cuba y Colombia, como también algunos de Argentina y Chile. En cambio, las mismas librerías no ofrecen ediciones originales de las revistas culturales ecuatorianas.

Un aspecto interesante, no sólo para la realización del proyecto, sino también para la investigación de la recepción de las revistas culturales latinoamericanas, es que, frecuentemente, se pueden adquirir títulos argentinos en Brasil, como *Para Ti* y *El Hogar*, así como algunos números de revistas chilenas en Buenos Aires, como *Selecta*.

Paralelamente a la adquisición, el IAI se encarga de la catalogación y clasificación formal y del análisis de las revistas, y de iniciar la digitalización de las revistas impresas. El personal bibliotecario del IAI lleva a cabo todas las labores de adquisición, catalogación y clasificación, junto con el resto de sus tareas. El núcleo del equipo lo componen los bibliógrafos responsables de los respectivos países; cuatro catalogadores, de los cuales tres se encargan de las ediciones impresas y en microfilm, y uno de la edición digital; una especialista en digitalización, metadatos y datos estructurales, y una encuadernadora. La DFG ha estado financiando, desde hace tres años, a una operadora de escaneado, encargada de escanear los ejemplares. Adicionalmente, se hacen pedidos de escaneado a empresas especializadas.

Las normas de buenas prácticas de digitalización de la DFG (www.dfg. de/formulare/12_151/12_151_en.pdf) constituyen la base del trabajo tanto de este como de todos los restantes proyectos de digitalización del IAI. La digitalización sólo se lleva a cabo después de una meticulosa pesquisa, en la que se trata de averiguar si la revista ya se ha convertido al formato digital en algún otro lugar. De ser así, se intenta, en la medida de lo posible, ofrecer un enlace de la copia digital localizada. Así se ha procedido, por ejemplo, en el caso de la revista argentina *Caras y Caretas*, con un enlace a la respectiva copia digital de la Biblioteca Nacional de España.

Puesta a disposición de los resultados

Las revistas retrodigitalizadas estarán accesibles al público en una plataforma de presentación, disponible en alemán, inglés y español, a la que se puede acceder a través de la sección "Colecciones Digitales" en el menú izquierdo de la página web del IAI o entrando directamente a www.iaidigital.de. Las búsquedas pueden realizarse en las Colecciones Digitales o a través del catálogo en línea OPAC del IAI; en este último caso, preferiblemente a partir de un título concreto. Mientras en OPAC pueden encontrarse todas las revistas culturales del proyecto, independientemente del formato físico en que estén disponibles, las Colecciones Digitales se limitan a las copias digitales realizadas por el IAI con sus propios fondos bibliotecarios.

Por lo tanto, la revista argentina *Caras y Caretas*, por ejemplo, no aparecerá en las Colecciones Digitales, pero sí en el OPAC del IAI, en el cual existe un enlace de la correspondiente copia digital en la Biblioteca Nacional de España. Por el contrario, *El Hogar, Plus Ultra* y *La Nota*, por citar tres ejemplos, aparecen tanto en el OPAC como en las Colecciones Digitales, puesto que su digitalización se llevó a cabo en el IAI.

Las copias digitales pertenecientes a las Colecciones Digitales del IAI pueden accederse gratuitamente en todo el mundo sin necesidad de ningún tipo de inscripción ni registro. No obstante, abrir una cuenta de usuario, independientemente de si se es o no un usuario registrado de la Biblioteca del Instituto Ibero-Americano, permite, entre otros servicios, usar módulos de colaboración abierta (*crowdsourcing*), grabar búsquedas y resultados de búsquedas, organizar una estantería virtual y hacer comentarios, que, por cierto, estamos deseosos de leer. Esperamos que los usuarios aporten información que nos permita seguir profundizando en la clasificación y contextualización de las revistas.

Lamentablemente, todavía no podemos ofrecer búsquedas de texto completo en las copias digitales.

Perspectivas

Esperamos concluir el proyecto a mediados del año 2016, pero como resultado de la acogida positiva alcanzada en la comunidad científica alemana e internacional, está previsto presentar una solicitud de extensión a la DFG. El objetivo sería incluir tanto nuevos títulos de los países ya integrados en el proyecto como también revistas culturales de otros países, como Brasil y Colombia.

Entre tanto y hasta donde lo permitan los fondos del IAI, ya se están aceptando ofertas de nuevos títulos que todavía no forman parte del proyecto. En este punto, vuelven a hacerse fundamentales los viajes de adquisición del IAI, en los que, casi sin excepción, se siguen descubriendo títulos que, o bien no están entre los fondos del IAI, o bien están presentes exclusivamente en colecciones incompletas.

También seguimos realizando interesantes hallazgos en esta área gracias a los proyectos de canje con socios selectos, como la Benson Collection de la University of Texas at Austin y la Latin American Collection de la Tulane University.

En el futuro, deseamos también potenciar la cooperación directa de investigación, especialmente en lo relacionado con el desarrollo conjunto de proyectos científicos. De igual forma, aspiramos a colaborar estrechamente con bibliotecas de Estados Unidos y América Latina, sobre todo en vista de las posibilidades ofrecidas por la digitalización cooperativa, cuyos componentes teóricos y prácticos ya estamos abordando intensamente en el IAI.

APÉNDICE

Lista de las revistas incluidas en el proyecto

Título de la revista	Lugar	Periodo de la publicación
Argentina		
ABC: Revista Semanal de Literatura Amena y Variada	Buenos Aires	1914
América en el Plata: Magazín Americano; Revista Mensual Continental	Buenos Aires	1907–1908
América Hispana: Revista Mensual Ilustrada	Buenos Aires	1920
Atlanta: Magazín Mensual	Buenos Aires	1911–1914
Atlántica: Revista Ilustrada y de Ideas	Buenos Aires	1925–1927
Atlántida: Ciencias, Letras, Arte, Historia Americana, Administración	Buenos Aires	1911–1914
Atlántida	Buenos Aires	1918–1970
Azul: Vida Social, Moda, Arte, Literatura	La Plata	1926
La Campana de Palo	Buenos Aires	1925–1927
Caras y Caretas	Buenos Aires	1898–
Céltiga: Revista Gallega de Arte, Crítica, Literatura y Actualidades	Buenos Aires	1924–1932
Claridad: Revista de Arte, Crítica y Letras; Tribuna Americana del Pensamiento Libre	Buenos Aires	1926–1941
La Esfera	Buenos Aires	1914–1919
Fantasio: Revista Mensual Ilustrada	Buenos Aires	1922–1924
Fray Mocho: Semanario Literario, Artístico y de Actualidades	Buenos Aires	1912–1929
El Gladiador: Semanario Ilustrado	Buenos Aires	1902–1924
El Hogar	Buenos Aires	1904–1958

Título de la revista	Lugar	Periodo de la publicación
Martín Fierro: Revista Popular de Crítica y Arte	Buenos Aires	1904–1905
Mate Amargo: Revista Semanal Ilustrada, Noticiosa, Instructiva y de Actualidades, Metropolitana y de las Provincias	Buenos Aires	1911
Mundo Argentino: La Revista para Toda la República; Notas de Actualidad	Buenos Aires	1910–[?]
Mundo Estudiantil: Revista Quincenal Ilustrada	Buenos Aires	1915
Nativa	Buenos Aires	1924–1973
Nosotros	Buenos Aires	1907–1943
La Nota: Revista Semanal	Buenos Aires	1915–1921
Orientación: Revista Mensual	Buenos Aires	1928–1929
Para Ti: Todo Para la Mujer	Buenos Aires	1922–1995
PBT: Alegre, Política, Deportiva	Buenos Aires	1904–1955
Plus Ultra	Buenos Aires	1916–1930
Sherlock Holmes: Revista Semanal Ilustrada	Buenos Aires	1911–1913
La Vida Moderna: Semanario; Magazín Argentino	Buenos Aires	1907–1912
Vida Porteña: Semanario; Magazín Argentino	Buenos Aires	1913–1922

Chile

Título de la revista	Lugar	Periodo de la publicación
El Acrata: Revista Quincenal de Sociología, Ciencia y Arte	Santiago de Chile	1900–1901
Atenea: Revista Mensual de Ciencias, Letras y Artes	Concepción	1924–1974
Chile Moderno: Revista Mensual	Valparaíso	1903
Pacífico Magazine: Revista Ilustrada Mensual	Santiago de Chile	1913–1921
Patria: Semanario Ilustrado	Santiago de Chile	1912
Revista de Artes y Letras: Revista Que Continúa la de "Los Diez"	Santiago de Chile	1917–1918
Revista Chilena: Diplomacia, Política, Historia, Artes, Letras	Santiago de Chile	1917–1930
La Revista de Chile: Publicación Quincenal	Santiago de Chile	1898–1901
Selecta: Revista Mensual Literaria y Artística	Santiago de Chile	1909–1912

Título de la revista	Lugar	Periodo de la publicación
La Tromba: Semanario de Sociología, Ciencias, Arte, Filosofía, Socialismo, Variedades y Actualidad	Santiago de Chile	1898
Cuba		
Alma Cubana: Historia, Literatura, Arte, Crítica	La Habana	1923–1926
Cervantes: Revista Mensual Ilustrada	La Habana	1925–1946
Cuba y América: Revista Mensual Ilustrada	La Habana	1897–1912
Cuba Contemporánea: Revista Mensual	La Habana	1913–1927
Cultura: Revista de Difusión Literaria, de Artes y Ciencias	Manzanillo	[?]–1925
Renacimiento	La Habana	1927–[?]
Revista de Cuba: Periódico Mensual de Ciencias, Derecho, Literatura y Bellas Artes	La Habana	1877–1884
Revista Cubana: Periódico Mensual de Ciencias, Filosofía, Literatura y Bellas Artes	La Habana	1885–1895
Revista de La Habana: Letras, Artes, Ciencias, Historia, Cuestiones Sociales	La Habana	1930
Revista Popular Cubana	La Habana	1907
Ecuador		
América Latina: Revista de Unión Latinoamericana	Cuenca	1924
Ciencias y Letras: Revista Mensual	Guayaquil	1912–1913
Dios y Patria: Revista de Cultura General	Riobamba	1923–1927
Entelequia: Órgano de la Sociedad Estudios Sociales	Quito	1927
Espirales: La Revista Moderna	Quito	1927–1930
Iniciación: Revista Literaria; Órgano del Centro Intelectual Bolívar	Tulcán	1925[?]
La Revista Ecuatoriana	Quito	1889–1894
Revista De Quito	Quito	1898
Semana Gráfica: Revista Ilustrada; Información, Arte, Literatura	Guayaquil	1931–1939
La Unión Literaria: Revista Mensual	Cuenca	1893–1938

Título de la revista	Lugar	Periodo de la publicación
Perú		
Actualidades: Revista Ilustrada	Lima	1903–1908
Almanaque de "El Comercio"	Lima	1892–1931
Amauta: Revista Mensual de Doctrina, Literatura, Arte, Polémica	Lima	1926–1930
El Cosmos: Periódico Científico, Literario	Arequipa	1892–1893
Ilustración Peruana	Lima	1909–1913
Mercurio Peruano: Revista Mensual de Ciencias Sociales y Letras	Lima	1918–
Mundial: Revista Semanal Ilustrada	Lima	1920–1933
Nueva Revista Peruana	Lima	1929–1930
El Perú Ilustrado: Semanario Para las Familias	Lima	1887
Prisma: Revista Ilustrada de Artes y Letras	Lima	1905–1907
Revista Americana	Lima	1863
La Revista de Lima: Periódico Quincenal	Lima	1860–1963
La Revista Semanal	Lima	1927
Variedades: Revista Semanal Ilustrada	Lima	1905–1932
Puerto Rico		
Brújula: Revista Cultural Puertorriqueña	San Juan	1934–1937
La Gaceta de Puerto Rico	San Juan	1806–1902
Heraldo Español	San Juan	1900
Índice: Mensuario de Historia, Literatura, Arte y Ciencia	San Juan	1929–1931
Pica-Pica	San Juan	1908–1943
Puerto Rico Ilustrado	San Juan	1910–1952

11. From Clueless to *Compadre*: SALALM, When the Sessions Are Over

Paula Covington

Mark Grover and David Block suggested that I add to their more serious remarks, some "anecdotes" about earlier times.[1] I thought that over and decided against it. Too many of those folks might never speak to me again! However, then I thought of some of the comments made on the recent survey on SALALM's structure, mission, activities, and utility. An anecdote or two may in fact be relevant. My first SALALM conference in the 1970s was an eye-opening experience, and three impressions stand out.

First, there were so many bright, knowledgeable, articulate, truly amazing people engaged in our efforts. Second, there was so much to be learned that getting a handle on this sort of task was going to be a true challenge. Third, and strongest, was how willing these brilliant people were to share. It was obvious that collaboration was one of the strong features of this group. Responses to the recent survey attest to this, with comments about the value of attending SALALM, such as: "There's no substitute for meeting with colleagues, exchanging ideas, planning the future." Another is that it's "the most important conference for my professional development." Still another responds it's the "only place I can talk about my work."

This probably should not have been a surprise. Before I interviewed for the Latin American position at Vanderbilt, I had already benefited from the aid of one of SALALM's best and brightest. I was in London for several months and spent time at the Institute for Latin American Studies "shadowing" Pat Noble, the Latin American librarian at the University of London Senate House Library. I read her detailed field trip reports, which had invaluable advice, including interesting tips on how to get out of jail if arrested in Managua. She encouraged me to attend SALALM if I were hired at Vanderbilt.

At my first SALALM there were attendees from many countries doing wonderful things. Marietta Daniels Shepard of the Pan American Union spoke about working with NASA and the National Library of Venezuela to use satellite transmissions for OCLC collaboration. She also presented on projects in Latin America to improve the development and production of books. A host of distinguished librarians from libraries in Latin America, Europe, and the US,

Who Are We Really?: Latin American Family, Local and Micro-Regional Histories, and Their Impact on Understanding Ourselves. Papers of the Fifty-Ninth Annual Meeting of SALALM, 2014.

including the Library of Congress, seemed to know each other. It was as if they lived in a private special world set apart from day-to-day routine. The theme of the conference was perfect for a relatively clueless beginner to the field: "The Multifaceted Role of the Latin American Bibliographer." During Anne Hartness and Laura Gutierrez-Witt's panel on these varied roles, I took notes madly. Up until that point I'd had little or no advice on making acquisitions with a large grant and a deadline. Finally, I was getting some practical guidance. In the recent survey, someone commented on SALALM conferences as "the one chance each year to meet with colleagues," and, to repeat the above, another noted it as "the only place I can talk about my work." That was definitely the case for me, especially in the pre-e-mail era when all acquisition work and other correspondence was by snail mail.

The other standout at that meeting was Barbara Valk. She was trying to organize a group to create an index to scholarly periodicals on Latin America—which continues to this day as the *Hispanic American Periodicals Index* (HAPI). It's hard to believe now, but scholars had no access to these materials. They had to depend on their own networks and whatever selected references to journal articles were included in the *Handbook of Latin American Studies*, by leafing through dozens of its annual volumes. My only prior experience with professional meetings was attending sessions of the American Library Association, in which I served on committees preoccupied with constantly rewriting their committee mission statements. Here instead was a pragmatic project fulfilling a real need, one of the first collaborative efforts that many "SALALMis" undertook. Everyone who worked with Barbara will remember her professionalism, organizational skills, passion for HAPI, and ability to get a group on board.

Experiences just before and after SALALM meetings have been equally educational. An exceptional one was a field trip to Nicaragua in 1983 for ten of us prior to the SALALM meeting in San José, Costa Rica. The week was organized by Ernesto Cardenal's Ministry of Culture, for he wanted us to see the *nueva Nicaragua* under the Sandinistas. We also wanted to explore ways to collaborate with or assist newly appointed university librarians. Many of them had received training with Dan Hazen when he taught there on a Fulbright, and were committed to developing libraries for the public and the Sandinista literacy campaign, but had few resources.

A week before we were scheduled to leave, Nicaragua expelled three US diplomats and, in response, the US closed all Nicaraguan consulates in the United States. The day I left, Comandante Tomás Borge, the only surviving member and leader of the original Frente Sandinista de Liberación Nacional (FSLN), and Nicaragua's minister of the interior, announced that visas would no longer be required for US citizens who wished to visit. We were nonetheless advised by the State Department not to go. It was a tense trip, but the Ministry of Culture had planned a full schedule of visits to libraries and universities, and receptions with poets and other distinguished Nicaraguans. Most of us hoped to get a free moment to locate the prolific revolutionary literature, political propaganda, and wealth of poetry and polemics being produced but previously inaccessible.

Each day one or two of us would disappear from the schedule. Dolores Martin of the Library of Congress was interviewing poets. Peter Johnson was looking for ephemera, as usual, especially in garages and other spots that distributed subversive political party pamphlets. I had a friend of a friend with a truck, who used his month's gas ration to drive me to various shops and agencies. We were followed by an agent of the CIA or some related agency, who was so inept that I finally told him where we were going next. Again, collaboration was the key with those SALALMis sneaking off to buy multiple copies for their colleagues in crime.

We ended our stay with the momentous appearance of Tomás Borge, who arrived unannounced at a reception and dinner. He kept us well into the night discussing his political philosophy and, when a member from the Library of Congress suggested we had a very early plane to catch, he suggested he would keep us in Nicaragua since we had not been fully converted. He was then given a brief, acerbic lecture by that colleague about his totalitarian practices, much to the consternation of the rest of us.

We flew out early the next morning, but only after dealing with problems of stolen tickets and our inability to use US credit cards in the country, not to mention the military's threat to impound our boxes of books. At the last moment, we were treated royally by the Ministry of Culture and all problems were waived. San José proved to be a "frying pan into the fire" experience. A bomb had gone off in front of our conference hotel in San José, followed by a 7.6 earthquake and many aftershocks. I remember Howard Karno suggesting it might be the subway beneath us. A subway? In Costa Rica? Inside, Marietta Daniels Shepard was still holding forth on her topic. As the chandeliers were swaying, the alarm clock on the podium went off, the usual way to stop her going overboard. As the room swayed, she simply reached over, reset it for another ten minutes and kept on talking.

We all have many educational experiences told or untold, the quirky travel exploits surrounding SALALM. It is no surprise that Ariel Dorfman, after having heard wacky though true tales of SALALMis, came to a SALALM meeting with the intention of writing about it. When he showed up I silently recalled various memories, such as of the five savvy Latin American booksellers who were flipped into a ditch on Copacabana and robbed the first night of our 1990 conference in Rio; of one member who broke a bottle of *cachaça* on the stone floor of the lobby of Rio's elegant Hotel Meridien and left behind aromas that wafted through three levels for hours.

At the end of that SALALM, a group of us started out to visit some of Brazil's major cultural sites. The first afternoon we found ourselves stranded in front of the gas pumps at a new Esso station in Rio, when the key broke in the ignition of our rental car. A barefoot, furry, yellow-striped "Tony the Tiger" danced while a small band played "When the Saints Go Marching In," to entice customers who couldn't use the pumps because of our car. The owner was none too happy with us. It was Sunday and a World Cup day for Brazil. Everything was closed, including the agency where we had picked up the car. Two of the group found a cab willing to go into a favela to find a *chaveiro* who made a rudimentary key while we commiserated with the overheated Tony and the gas station owner. Robert McNeil, being British, managed to find a pub across the street with takeaways to help assuage them. We did make it to Ouro Preto that night, and the rest of the trip was as marvelous as we had hoped.

Another happy post-SALALM memory was riding horseback in Monteverde in Costa Rica with Eduardo Lozano, an expert horseman from the pampas, and Barbara Valk. As we galloped along a dirt road we came clattering into a small village. Casino doors opened from a bar and cowboys came out to observe the noise like a bad Western. We were all gleeful to be racing along with each other on horseback. Only Clint Eastwood was missing!

Ranging from book fairs to rainforest tours, pre- and post-SALALM memories of Latin America, and the friendships made during the conferences, have given so many of us a deeper appreciation and understanding of each nation's history, culture, society, and economy, in addition to its publishing patterns and practices.

And what of conferences in more recent years? What of conferences now? Sharing ideas about booksellers, learning the identity of emerging writers and scholars, exchanging ideas about how to overcome the lack of bibliographic control in countries where national libraries suffer from weak deposit laws, surely those are experiences common to everyone here, including those who attend a SALALM conference for the first time. At the end of my own first conference I was amazed at how much I had learned, both about books and institutions. I was even more amazed at the many important contacts I had made with book dealers and librarians, not only in the US but in Europe, Latin America, and even Australia. Especially in the era before the Internet, I knew this was more valuable than gold. I also learned that SALALM members were doing many exciting projects and they were passionate about their work.

One of the comments in the recent satisfaction survey was, "SALALM has provided me with much mentorship" from all generations of members. Such sharing, learning, and mentoring aren't just confined to the sessions themselves. All of us have gained many insights over a cup of coffee or a glass of wine. As my remarks indicate, many of us have taken things a bit further and enjoyed the friendship of our colleagues. I very much hope that this continues to be the case, in this year and the years ahead. Here in Salt Lake City, much attention is paid to exploring the histories of families. SALALM is a different kind of family, but no less close, no less supportive, whether it be librarians like my two fellow panelists, or booksellers like Howard Karno. We all learn to appreciate one another and learn one another's eccentricities, and we cannot wait for the opportunity to be together again for yet one more SALALM conference!

NOTE

1. This paper was part of a panel entitled "SALALM: Back in the Day" and also featured presentations by Grover and Block.

Contributors

CLAIRE-LISE BÉNAUD, University of New Mexico Libraries

PAULA COVINGTON, Vanderbilt University

SONIA DE LA CRUZ, University of Oregon

MARÍA DEL MAR GONZÁLEZ-GONZÁLEZ, California College of the Arts

STEPHANIE KAYS, University of Oregon

RICARDA MUSSER, Ibero-Amerikanisches Institut, Preußischer Kulturbesitz

BETSAIDA M. REYES, University of Kansas

NELSON SANTANA, The City College of New York

ANTONIO SOTOMAYOR, University of Illinois

RAFAEL E. TARRAGÓ, University of Minnesota

JUDITH E. TOPPIN, The University of the West Indies

DAVID WOKEN, University of Oregon

JOHN B. WRIGHT, Brigham Young University

Conference Program

Saturday, May 10

8am–5pm	Registration
8:30–10:30am	ARL Latin American Research Resources Project (LARRP)
10:30–11:30am	New Member Orientation
11:30am–1pm	*LUNCH*
1–3pm	*Regional Group Meetings* CALAFIA LANE LASER MOLLAS
3–4pm	Librarian/Bookdealer/Publisher Meeting Ibero-American Studies in SALALM (ISiS) Cataloging and Bibliographic Technologies Academic Latino/a Zone of Action and Research (ALZAR)
4–5pm	*Committee Meetings* Interlibrary Cooperation Nominating Constitution & Bylaws Medina Award
5–6pm	Welcome Happy Hour for New Members & ENLACE *Becarios*
7:30–9:30pm	Latin American Microforms Project (LAMP)

Sunday, May 11

8am–5pm	Registration
8:30am	Meet in Lobby to walk to Choir Broadcast
9–10am	Mormon Tabernacle Choir Broadcast
10am	Walk back to hotel
10:30–11:30am	*Committee Meetings* Marginalized Peoples & Ideas Electronic Resources Hispanic American Periodicals Index (HAPI) Cuban Bibliography
11:30am–1pm	*Committee Meetings* Reference and Bibliographic Instruction Services Finance #1 (Finance #2 will be held Tuesday, May 13, 7–8am) *Libreros*

1–2:30pm	*LUNCH*
2:30–6pm	*Libreros*/Librarians Consultations
2:30–3:30pm	*Committee Meetings* Communications ENLACE Audio Visual/Media
3:30–4:30pm	*Committee Meetings* Editorial Board Membership Serials Policy, Research & Investigation (PRI)
4:30–6:30pm	Executive Board #1 (EB #2, Wed., May 14, 3:30–5pm) Rapporteur: **Craig Schroer**, University of West Georgia
8–10pm	Discussion: SALALM and the Program for Latin American Libraries and Archives

Monday, May 12

8am–5pm	Registration
8:30–9am	**Opening Session** Rapporteur: **Molly E. Molloy**, New Mexico State University
	Welcome Remarks
	Roberto C. Delgadillo, SALALM President 2013–14, University of California, Davis
	Jennifer F. Paustenbaugh, University Librarian, Brigham Young University
	John B. Wright, Local Arrangements Chair
	José Toribio Medina Award presented by Roberto C. Delgadillo
9–10am	**Opening Keynote Address**
	Lynn Turner, FamilySearch *FamilySearch's Latin American Records Collection—* *Past, Present, and Future* Introduction: **Roberto C. Delgadillo**, University of California, Davis Rapporteur: **Molly E. Molloy**, New Mexico State University
10–10:30am	*Book Exhibits Opening Reception* *Coffee Break*
10:30am–12pm	**Panel 1—Roda Viva I: Emerging Trends and Practices** Moderator: **Alison Hicks**, University of Colorado, Boulder Rapporteur: **Nathalie Soini**, Queen's University
	Presenters:
	Antonio Sotomayor, University of Illinois at Urbana-Champaign *Opening the Vault of Eighteenth Century Andean History: A Portal to* *the Conde de Montemar Letters at the University of Illinois' Library* *(1761–1799)*

Betsaida M. Reyes, University of Kansas
*The Value of Family Ties: How Mentorship Relations Can Help You
Succeed in Your Career*

Christine Hernández, Tulane University
The Latin American Library's Special Collections in Digital

D. Ryan Lynch, Knox College
*Looking for an Opening: The Role (or Lack Thereof) of Librarians in
Knox College's First-Year Seminars*

Bronwen Maxson, Davis Graham & Stubbs LLP
5 Things I Learned During the Novela Mundial Digitization Project

Jill E. Baron, Dartmouth College
*Portuguese-Language Films at Dartmouth (PLFD) Guide:
A Digital Learning and Discovery Tool*

Sara Levinson, University of North Carolina at Chapel Hill
*What Do I Do Now? Strategies for Providing Access to Library
Materials in Languages You Don't Know*

10:30am–12pm   **Panel 2—Mapping and Visualizing Collections for Local Histories
and a Genealogical Case Study**
Moderator: **Georgette Dorn**, Library of Congress
Rapporteur: **David Dressing**, University of Notre Dame

Presenters:

Rhonda Neugebauer, University of Calfornia, Riverside

Shonn M. Haren, University of Calfornia, Riverside
*Collection Mapping and Data Visualization as Tools for Collection
Development and Collection Assessment: The Latin American Studies
Collection at the University of California, Riverside*

Paul S. Losch, University of Florida
The Panama Canal Museum Collection at the University of Florida

Judith Toppin, University of the West Indies, Cave Hill Campus
*Linkages, Lineage, and Kinship in the Anglo-Caribbean Family
Experience: A Genealogical Case Study*

10:30am–12pm   **Panel 3—The Family in Cuban History and Culture**
Moderator: **Rafael E. Tarragó**, University of Minnesota
Rapporteur: **Theresa E. Polk**, University of Maryland, College Park,
                         graduate student

Presenters:

Rafael E. Tarragó, University of Minnesota
*From the Colony to the Republic: Bibliographic Notes on
Entrepreneurial Dynasties in Cuba*

Meiyolet Méndez, University of Miami
*Ties That Bind: The Fernando Fernández-Cavada Papers at the Cuban
Heritage Collection*

Martha E. Mantilla, University of Pittsburgh
*My Intriguing Encounter with Julio Elizalde's Manuscripts: The Case of
a Micro-Family History of a Cuban in Exile*

12:00–1:15pm   *LUNCH*

1:15pm	Load onto Buses
1:30–2:30pm	Trip to Brigham Young University

2:45–4:15pm — **Panel 4—The Latin American Family and Community: Depictions and Representations**
Moderator: **Mark L. Grover**, Brigham Young University, *retired*
Rapporteur: **Gabriella Reznowski**, Washington State University

Presenters:

Doug Weatherford, Brigham Young University
Populating the Margins: The Struggles of Families and Communities in The Milk of Sorrow *by Claudia Llosa*

Rex Nielson, Brigham Young University
Socially Rooted Authoritarianism in Lygia Fagundes Telles' As Meninas

Library Tour/Special Collections Presentation

4:30–5:30pm	*Host Reception*
5:45–6:45pm	Travel to Park City
6:45–9:30pm	Park City for no-host dinner
9:30pm	Buses depart from Park City to hotel

Tuesday, May 13

7–8am	Finance Committee Meeting #2
8am–5pm	Registration
8am–5pm	**Book Exhibits**

8–9:30am — **Panel 5—Ebooks en Español: New Developments**
Moderator: **Adán Griego**, Stanford University
Rapporteur: **Virginia García**, Instituto de Estudios Peruanos

Presenters:

Kathryn Paoletti, Casalini libri

Lluis Claret, Digitalia

Leslie Lees, e-libro/ebrary

Fernando Genovart, Librería García Cambeiro

Frank Smith, JSTOR

8–9:30am — **Panel 6—Cataloging, Bibliographic Control and Library Services**
Moderator: **Daniel Schoorl**, HAPI
Rapporteur: **Meiyolet Méndez**, University of Miami

Presenters:

Brenda Salem, University of Pittsburgh
Finding Your History in the Library Catalog: How Subject Analysis Can Improve Access to Family and Local Histories

Timothy A. Thompson, University of Miami
Mairelys Lemus-Rojas, University of Miami
Bringing Cuban Theater Collections to Wikipedia with the RAMP (Remixing Archival Metadata Project) Editor

John B. Wright, Brigham Young University
What's in a Name: Families as Creators

8–9:30am   **Panel 7—What We Talk About, When We Talk About "Familia"**
Moderator: **D. Ryan Lynch**, Knox College
Rapporteur: **Jennifer Osorio**, University of California, Los Angeles

Presenters:

Sócrates Silva, University of California, Santa Barbara
La Familia: Documenting LGBTQ Student Networks in Higher Education

Michael Scott, Georgetown University
Contad@s: Data Sources on LGBT-Headed Families in Latin America

Melissa Gasparotto, Rutgers University
Uncovering the US Latina Lesbian Genealogy

9:30–10am   *Coffee Break*

10–11:30am   **Panel 8—Professional Development Outside of SALALM**
Moderator: **Adán Griego**, Stanford University
Rapporteur: **Anne Barnhart**, University of West Georgia

Presenters:

Adán Griego, Stanford University
Involvement with ALA & Attending International Book Fairs

Alison Hicks, University of Colorado, Boulder
Participation at International Library Conferences

Orchid Mazurkiewicz, HAPI
Indexing for HAPI and MLA

10–11:30am   **Panel 9—Documenting and Defining: The Role of Documentary Projects in Helping Communities Define Themselves**
Moderator: **D. Ryan Lynch**, Knox College
Rapporteur: **David Woken**, University of Oregon

Presenters:

Eduardo A. Ortiz, Utah State University
Cache Valley Utah Latino Voices and History

Fahina Tavake-Pasi, National Tongan American Society
Pacific Islanders: Our Past, Key to a Healthier Future

Leslie G. Kelen, Center for Documentary Expression and Art
Documentary and Ethnic Identity: Challenges and Possibilities

D. Ryan Lynch, Knox College
Strange Bedfellows: How a Science Museum, a State Agency, and Local Organizers Made It Possible to Re-Write Rochester, New York's History

10–11:30am   **Panel 10—The Other Latin@s: The Dominican and Puerto Rican Experience—Collections and Resources**
Moderator: **Jennifer Osorio**, University of California, Los Angeles
Rapporteur: **Christine Hernández**, Tulane University

Presenters:

Sarah Aponte, CUNY Dominican Studies Institute Archive &
The City College of New York Libraries
*The Building of an Academic Dominican Library: Impact at the
Local Level and Beyond*

Nelson Santana, CUNY Dominican Studies Institute Archives &
The City College of New York Libraries
*Introduction to the Intellectual History of Dominican Migration in the
United States*

María del Mar González-González, University of Utah,
post-doctoral fellow
*Identity Politics and Puerto Rican Visual Resources:
Notes from the Field*

11:30am–1:30pm   *NO-HOST LUNCHES*

1:30–3pm   **Town Hall Meeting**
Rapporteur: **Craig Schroer**, University of West Georgia

3–4:30pm   **Panel 11—Roda Viva II: Even More Emerging Trends and Practices**
Moderator: **Alison Hicks**, University of Colorado, Boulder
Rapporteur: **Melissa Gasparotto**, Rutgers University

Presenters:

Paula Covington, Vanderbilt University
*Latin American Digital Projects: Student, Faculty and Library
Collaborations at Vanderbilt University*

Anne Barnhart, University of West Georgia
*Because Learning Is Not Just for Students: Information Literacy
for Faculty*

Sarah Buck Kachaluba, Florida State University
*Follow Up to "From Dumb Assessment to Smart Assessment":
Adaptions for FSU Libraries*

Suzanne M. Schadl, University of New Mexico
*Tagging ASARO: A UNM Experiment in Crowd-Sourcing and
Collection Development*

Daisy V. Domínguez, The City College of New York Libraries (CUNY)
Teach With Music

Molly E. Molloy, New Mexico State University
The Femicide Fallacy

Barbara Alvarez, University of Michigan
*Don Quixote in English: A Chronology: A Digital Humanities Project
for the Classroom*

3–4:30pm   **Panel 12—Families across Borders: Unique Collections and
Special Projects Linking South Westerners with Latin Americans**
Moderator: **Wendy Pedersen**, University of New Mexico
Rapporteur: **Michael Scott**, Georgetown University

Presenters:

Paulita Aguilar, University of New Mexico
*Cultural Connections between a Zapotecan Village, Teotitlan del Valle,
and New Mexico Pueblos: Imagined or Real?*

Claire-Lise Bénaud, University of New Mexico
Ordinary Images: Appreciating Photographs of Children in a Pictorial Archive

Suzanne M. Schadl, University of New Mexico
Michael Hoopes, University of New Mexico
All in the Family: Special Collections Digitally Born

3–4:30pm   **Panel 13—Identidades y Voces Múltiples Desde México y América Central**

Moderator: **Wendy Griffin**, formerly at Universidad Pedagógica Nacional FranciscoMorazán (UPNFM) and www.hondurasweekly.com
Rapporteur: **Sócrates Silva**, University of California, Santa Barbara

Presenters:

Nora Domínguez Rodríguez, Instituto Centroamericano de Estudios Sociales y Desarrollo (INCEDES) e Instituto Guatemalteco Americano (IGA)
Rosa Elvira Cedillo Villar, Instituto Nacional para la Evaluación de la Educación, México
Los Migrantes que se Van, las Familias que se Quedan. ¿Qué Mantiene los Lazos que los Une?

Wendy Griffin, formerly at UPNFM and www.hondurasweekly.com
Diásporas Mulitiples: Las Historias de las Familias de 6 Autores Afro-Hondureños con Conexiones a Nueva York, Atlanta, Miami, Chicago, y Hartford, Connecticut

Lázaro Flores, UPNFM, *jubilado*
Wendy Griffin, formerly at UPNFM and www.hondurasweekly.com
Identidades Múltiples: Los Orígenes y Las Luchas del Dr. Lázaro Flores, el Primer Antropólogo Lenca en Honduras, Autor, Activista, y Formador de Hondureños e Investigadores Nacionales e Internacionales con Conciencia e Identidad

4:30–6pm   **Panel 14—Tendencias Editoriales y Realidades Libreras Latinoamericanas**
Moderator: **Alvaro J. Risso**, Librería Linardi y Risso
Rapporteur: **Wendy Pedersen**, University of New Mexico

Presenters:

Julio Marchena, Libros Peruanos S.A.
Nuevas Tendencias en la Industria Editorial Peruana

Fernando Genovart, Librería García Cambeiro
Argentinean Academic Publishing Industry, Monographs

Vera de Araujo-Shellard, Susan Bach Books from Brazil
Sandra Soares de Costa, Susan Bach Books from Brazil
Publishing Trends in Contemporary Brazil: Who is Minding the Book Store?

S. Lief Adleson, Books from Mexico
Pedro Figueroa, Books from Mexico
Among Books and Dealers: Constants and Changes in the Mexican Academic Publishing Industry

S. Lief Adleson, Books from Mexico
Preliminary Report of the Acquisitions Trends Survey Task Force

4:30–6pm	**Panel 15—New and Continuing Voices in the SALALM Family I** Moderator: **Melissa Gasparotto**, Rutgers University Rapporteur: **Irene Münster**, Universities at Shady Grove

Presenters:

Monica Lozano, The University of Texas at Austin, *graduate student*
Creating Identity: Through Oral History and Storytelling

Theresa E. Polk, University of Maryland, College Park,
graduate student
Until We Find Them: Disappearance, State Records, and the
Right to Truth

Luis A. González, Indiana University
A Book, a Translator, and a Publisher: An Intellectual Family Story

Sarah Buck Kachaluba, Florida State University
A SALALMista Testimonial: From Teaching Professor to Academic
Librarian, Combining Research in History and Librarianship, and
Digital Humanities

7–10pm	*Libreros' Reception*

Wednesday, May 14

8am–5pm	Registration
8am–3pm	**Book Exhibits**
8–9:30am	**Panel 16—Family History Opportunities at** **Brigham Young University** Moderator: **Jill N. Crandell**, Center for Family History and Genealogy, Brigham Young University Rapporteur: **Barbara Miller**, California State University, Fullerton

Presenters:

Noel Maxfield, Digital Browse, FamilySearch
The Immigrant Ancestors Project

Paul Woodbury, BYU Family History Lab, *undergraduate student*
Introduction to Genetic Genealogy

Jill N. Crandell, Center for Family History and Genealogy,
Brigham Young University
The BYU Center for Family History and Genealogy

8–9:30am	**Panel 17—New and Continuing Voices in the SALALM Family II** Moderator: **Roberto C. Delgadillo**, University of California, Davis Rapporteur: **Nelmy Jerez**, University of New Mexico

Presenters:

Antonio Sotomayor, University of Illinois at Urbana-Champaign
Challenges to Caribbean Family History and Genealogy: Archives,
Sources, and Oral History in Puerto Rico

David Woken, University of Oregon, Eugene
Sonia de la Cruz, University of Oregon, Eugene
Stephanie Kays, University of Oregon, Eugene
Latino History is Oregon History: Preserving Oregon's Latino Heritage
through the Pineros y Campesinos Unidos del Noroeste Archive

Carlos Gazzera, Presidente de la Red de Editoriales de Universidades Nacionales (REUN)
El Libro Universitario Argentino: Presente y Futuro

Nelmy Jerez, University of New Mexico
LADB—An Electronic Resource on Latin America

8–9:30am   **Panel 18—The Role of Collecting Diaries, Journals and Photographs for Genealogical Research: Case Studies**
Moderator: **Donna Canevari de Paredes**, University of Saskatchewan
Rapporteur: **Jill E. Baron**, Dartmouth College

Presenters:

John B. Wright, Brigham Young University
Discovering Self through Ancestors' Diaries

Peter Altekrüger, Ibero-Amerikanisches Institut PK, Berlin
De Amor, Crimen y Cotidianidad. Las Revistas Teatrales y Colecciones de Novelas Cortas Argentinas del Instituto Ibero-Americano

Ricarda Musser, Ibero-Amerikanisches Institut PK, Berlin
Cultural Magazines of Latin America. An Acquisition and Digitalization Project of the Ibero-American Institute/Berlin

Silvana Jacqueline Aquino Remigio, Biblioteca España de la Artes del Centro Cultural de la Universidad Nacional Mayor de San Marcos, Peru
Las Fotografías como Fuente de Información Genealógica: Breve Mirada al Caso del Archivo Courret

9:30–10am   *Coffee Break*

10–11:30am   **Panel 19—FamilySearch.org in Latin America: Strategy Acquisition, Indexing and Research Methodologies**
Moderator: **Karina E. Morales**, FamilySearch
Rapporteur: **Daniel Schoorl**, HAPI

Presenters:

Karina E. Morales, FamilySearch
General Strategy for Acquiring and Negotiating Historical Records in Latin American Acquisition

Adele Marcum, FamilySearch
Preparing Records for Publication Online

Debbie Gurtler, FamilySearch
Research Methodology: A Librarian's Perspective

10–11:30am   **Panel 20—New and Continuing Approaches in the Training of SALALMistas**
Moderator: **Orchid Mazurkiewicz**, HAPI
Rapporteur: **D. Ryan Lynch**, Knox College

Presenters:

Alison Hicks, University of Colorado, Boulder
Bilingual Information in the Workplace: Preparing Undergraduates for Spanish/English Information Environments

Betsaida M. Reyes, University of Kansas
Shaping Students' Learning through Embedded Librarianship

Daisy V. Domínguez, The City College of New York Libraries (CUNY)
Animal Relations: Fostering Human-Animal Studies in Latin American History Collections

Melissa Gasparotto, Rutgers University
A Ten Year Analysis of Dissertation Bibliographies from the Department of Spanish and Portuguese at Rutgers University

10–11:30am   **Panel 21—SALALM: Back in the Day**
Moderator: **Gayle Williams**, Florida International University
Rapporteur: **Bridget Gazzo**, Dumbarton Oaks

Presenters:

Mark L. Grover, Brigham Young University, *retired*
How Peter T. Johnson Saved (or Ruined) SALALM: Transitions and the Future

David Block, The University of Texas at Austin
SALALM, Two Decades Ago

Paula Covington, Vanderbilt University
Clueless to Compadre: SALALM and when the Sessions are Over

11:30am–1:30pm   *NO-HOST LUNCHES*

1:30–2:30pm   **Closing Keynote Address**

Thomas K. Edlund, Brigham Young University
*The Why's and Why Not's of Family History Research:
A Professional's Retrospective*
Introduction: **Roberto C. Delgadillo**, University of California, Davis
Rapporteur: **David Block**, The University of Texas at Austin

2:30–3:30pm   Closing Session and Business Meeting
Rapporteur: **Suzanne M. Schadl**, University of New Mexico

3:30–5pm   Executive Board #2
Rapporteur: **Craig Schroer**, University of West Georgia

3pm   *Book Exhibits Close*